SNAKES
AND OTHER REPTILES
OF SOUTHERN AFRICA

BILL BRANCH

Dedication

To friends in the field, particularly Aaron, Johan, Colin, Werner, Randy, Paul, Trip, Mike, Krystal and MO: may many happy days we squander, and tomorrow always be a holiday!

Published by Struik Nature (an imprint of Penguin Random House
South Africa (Pty) Ltd)
Reg. No. 1953/000441/07
The Estuaries No. 4, Century Avenue (Oxbow Crescent), Century City, 7441
PO Box 1144, Cape Town, 8000 South Africa

Visit **www.randomstruik.co.za** and join the Struik Nature Club for updates, news, events and special offers

First published 1993 as *A Photographic Guide to Snakes and other Reptiles of Southern Africa*
Second edition 2001
Third reworked edition (*Pocket Guide: Snakes and other Reptiles of Southern Africa*) 2016

10 9 8 7 6 5 4 3 2 1

Publisher: Pippa Parker
Managing editor: Helen de Villiers
Editor: Colette Alves
Design director: Janice Evans
Designer: Neil Bester
Proofreader: Thea Grobbelaar

Reproduction: Hirt & Carter Cape (Pty) Ltd
Printing and binding: Times Offset (M) Sdn Bhd, Malaysia

Print: 978 1 77584 164 7
E-pub: 978 1 77584 377 1
E-PDF: 978 1 77584 378 8

Front cover: Boomslang; Title page: Giant Girdled Lizard; Back cover (top to bottom): Pygmy Wolf Snake, Cape Dwarf Chameleon (Krystal Tolley), Cape Crag Lizard

CONTENTS

INTRODUCTION

Web-footed Gecko *(Pachydactylus rangei)*

With increasing public concern for the environment, and the emergence of the 'citizen scientist', interest in less-fashionable wildlife such as reptiles and amphibians has increased. If we are to return to a state of harmony with our world, and to integrate with the biosphere rather than continually exploit it, then we need a deeper understanding of life around us. This book is designed to introduce the region's reptiles, from the feared snakes and crocodile to the ever-popular tortoises and the secretive and neglected lizards.

Southern Africa, that region south of the Zambezi and Kunene rivers, has a tremendous variety of habitats. These harbour a diverse reptile fauna of more than 600 species. Nearly 70% of these are endemic to the region, being found nowhere else. Obviously, not all of these can be included in this small book. The species chosen are those that are more colourful and conspicuous, as well as those unique to or endangered in southern Africa. However, a number of rare and localized species have also been included to reflect the great diversity of reptiles the region supports.

People generally realize that most snakes are not poisonous, but many still kill them, using the lazy argument that it is 'better to be safe than sorry'. However, of 168 snake species found in southern Africa, less than one-third have venoms of medical significance. Of these, 18 have probably caused death and a further 31 can deliver bites with symptoms ranging from mild to serious. Many regions have fewer than a handful of dangerous species, and it requires little effort to recognize these. All dangerous species are included in this guide.

Classification of reptiles

Living reptiles are an extremely diverse class, and the relationships of the main orders and families are still controversial. Four main lineages survive. The lizard-like tuataras (Order Rhynchocephalia) are restricted to New Zealand. The remaining three orders occur in southern Africa, including the crocodilians (Order Crocodylia), tortoises, terrapins and turtles

The Bicoloured Quill-snouted Snake *(Xenocalamus bicolor)* is an AfroMalagasy snake, a group that is unique to Africa.

(collectively called chelonians, Order Testudines), and snakes and lizards (collectively called squamates, Order Squamata). Crocodiles are more closely related to dinosaurs and birds than to other reptiles, while chelonians have little similarity to the other living reptiles. Squamates (scaled reptiles) are all closely related, with snakes evolving from lizards approximately 100 million years ago. Previously, worm lizards (amphisbaenids) were treated in similar fashion to snakes, as a squamate suborder of comparable level to lizards. This is inconsistent, as snakes are basically another form of legless lizard, and their classification should reflect this. The problem, however, is trying to shuffle the massive diversity of snakes (nearly 3,500 species worldwide) into the limited recognized taxonomic categories with lizards (families, subfamilies, genera, etc).

The grouping of snakes by their dentition, and the idea that this single feature reflects their evolution, is now outdated. Gene sequence studies have allowed much greater understanding of the true relationships between snakes and their biogeography. Africa is home to a group of unique snakes, the AfroMalagasy snakes (Family Lamprophiidae; i.e. lamprophid snakes – a simple term for the family, as with canids for dogs and felids for cats). These snakes evolved in Africa and most are endemic, but only a few are venomous. This family includes the familiar house snakes, sand snakes, burrowing asps and centipede-eaters, which are placed in different lamprophid subfamilies. Lamprophids are closely related to the much more venomous cobras and mambas (Family Elapidae). The other main group of venomous snakes, the adders and vipers (Family Viperidae), are relatively primitive snakes, although this refers to their genealogy and belies the sophistication of their complicated erectile front fangs.

Limb loss in lizards has evolved in many species, the most conspicuous being in snakes. It is not always easy to distinguish other legless lizards from snakes. Most snakes have enlarged belly scales (ventrals) that aid locomotion; no other legless lizard has these. Snakes and legless lizards require neither eyes to see nor enlarged ventral scales to move when living underground. The eyes of snakes, when present, lack eyelids and have an unblinking stare. In contrast, many legless lizards still retain eyelids. The two groups may look very similar, and there is no simple rule for telling them apart. However, all blind snakes have very short tails with a sharp spine at the tip. They also have rounder, blunter heads than any legless lizard.

Reptiles have limited mobility and many have very specific habitat requirements. In general, lizards can be considered habitat-linked and snakes food-linked. This is reflected in many of their common names. Thus, snakes have names such as egg-eaters, centipede-eaters and slug-eaters, whereas lizards have names such as desert lizards, rock lizards, and water monitor. In practical terms, this means that lizards often have very small ranges, within which they inhabit specific places. In contrast, snakes often range over large areas and occur in different habitats, but search for specific prey.

Reproduction

The majority of reptiles, including all crocodiles and chelonians, are oviparous (egg-laying). Most lay clutches of between 5 and 20 eggs, although large sea turtles may lay up to 1,000 eggs in a season; most geckos lay only two eggs at a time, and some lay only one. With few exceptions, parental care in local reptiles ends when the eggs are laid and the nest hole covered. The Southern African Python

A Cape Marsh Terrapin *(Pelomedusa galeata)* hatching from its shell.

and Nile Crocodile both brood their eggs until they hatch. In crocodiles and sea turtles the sex of the embryo is dependent upon the temperature at which the egg is incubated. In crocodiles, males develop in eggs at high temperatures, while the same temperatures in turtles produce females. Many squamates are viviparous, retaining their eggs within the body and giving birth to live young. This usually occurs in cool climates.

HOW TO USE THIS BOOK

Clarity and ease of use have been the main criteria in the design of this guide. Thumbnail silhouettes allow quick access to the appropriate reptile group. The size shown is total length, with the range from young adult to maximum size. In the succinct species descriptions, key features for identification are emphasized in italic type. In some difficult groups, such as thread snakes and sand lizards, it may be necessary to have the specimen in hand to obtain detailed scale counts before a positive identification can be assured. As with birds, field identification is not always easy and depends on sensible and good observation.

WHEN FIRST SPOTTING A REPTILE, NOTE THE FOLLOWING FEATURES:

- What was the general build?
- Was the coloration uniform or patterned? If patterned, was it plain, striped, blotched, etc.?
- Was the tail longer or shorter than the body?
- Were the body scales large or small, smooth or rough, arranged in rows, or scattered?
- What habitat was it in, and what was it doing?

These features should be jotted in a field book, as an aid for comparison with the pictures in the species accounts. A **glossary** of **specialized terms** and **diagrams** showing the anatomy of various reptiles is featured on pp.154–155.

When trying to match a species to a photograph in the book, check the map to see if the reptile occurs in the particular region. If there is a big difference between where you have found it and where it should be, try another species. Although many reptile distributions are poorly known, you are unlikely to discover major range extensions. It is more likely that you have simply misidentified the species. Remember that many species, particularly lizards, are not included in this guide. You are directed to a selection of further reading (p.154) that should facilitate identification of any unusual species.

Key to symbols used in this book

 Venomous snake whose bite can be fatal to humans

 Venomous snake whose bite is not known to be fatal

 Non-venomous snake that has killed people

CE Critically Endangered (extremely high risk of extinction in the wild)

E Endangered (high risk of extinction in the wild)

V Vulnerable (high risk of endangerment in the wild)

NT Near Threatened (likely to become endangered in the near future)

FIELD HINTS

The first requirement for field work is to wear suitable clothing: subdued in colour and robust enough to survive thorns and sharp rocks. Carry a good pair of compact binoculars, which can focus down to 2–3m, as well as a small pocket-sized notebook to record observations.

In most of southern Africa, provincial legislation prohibits the collecting, transport or possession of reptiles and amphibians. It is therefore illegal to catch them unless special permission has been obtained. It is also necessary to gain permission to walk or collect on private land. Given these restrictions, however, nothing prevents you from observing and enjoying reptiles in the wild. Bird-spotting is a pastime enjoyed by thousands of South Africans, and there is no reason why reptile-spotting cannot be as enjoyable.

Observing reptiles

Unlike birds, which are often common and highly visible, most reptiles are small, secretive and shy. To find or observe them usually requires patience and careful searching. When in the field, walk slowly and quietly, scanning the ground or rock outcrops ahead. Reptiles are ectotherms and gain their body heat externally, usually from basking in the sun. On cool days or in winter they are rarely active. Being small, they warm up quickly and then usually retreat to shade to avoid overheating and to be less visible to predators. On hot days, they are therefore best observed in the early morning and late afternoon. On overcast days they may be active all day. Observing need not be limited to daytime. Most geckos are nocturnal and gather at lights to catch the moths that they attract. Nocturnal snakes and some lizards crawl onto tarred roads in the early evening to absorb the residual heat from the sun-warmed surface. They can be spotted on quiet roads on warm evenings, particularly in spring. Chameleons are easier to find at night using a torch, as they turn pale and may sit in exposed positions.

Mating season is also a good time to observe reptiles. In the southern, more temperate regions, mating occurs in spring as daytime temperatures rise, while in the north it often occurs at the start of the wet season. Male snakes become more active at these times, searching for receptive females. Dominant males among colonial agamas, flat lizards and skinks develop bright breeding colours, and lead active lives defending their territories and chasing mates. Many lizards and tortoises have small home ranges in which they have one or several retreats that they use all their lives. The 'fright distance', the closest approach they will allow before retreating, is usually relatively small and well within the close range of normal binoculars. After several visits they often become habituated to the presence of an observer, and behave normally. You can then easily observe interesting territorial and mating displays.

Collecting reptiles

If you have permission to collect, you can locate many species in their shelters. Burrowing or nocturnal species can be uncovered by looking under boulders, rotting logs, grass piles, etc. Remember to return logs and rocks to their original position after looking under them. They provide essential shelter for many creatures, including reptiles, and care should be taken not to destroy this microhabitat. Terrestrial species may become trapped in holes such as storm-water culverts or cattle grids. Many burrowing species are exposed by farm ploughs or during bush clearance for roads, dams or new farmland.

Venomous snakes should always be caught with thick gloves, or a mechanical noose or grab-stick. Most other snakes and lizards can be caught simply by hand, although large pythons and monitor lizards can give powerful and painful bites. Many lizards shed their tail when grabbed, and so care should be taken if perfect specimens are desired. Lizards are better collected with a noose of fine cotton or wire attached to a telescopic fishing rod or radio aerial. Stronger nooses can be used to extract rock-living lizards from cracks. Fast-moving skinks and sand lizards can be stunned with rubber bands cut from an old car inner tube. These are simply hooked onto a finger, stretched, aimed and fired at the lizard. The effective distance is usually about 2m.

Red-lipped Snake *(Crotaphopeltis hotamboeia)* is not venomous but can give a powerful bite.

Reptiles may be found dead on roads, ploughed up during farming or road construction, or drowned in swimming pools. They can be preserved in formalin (10%) or methylated spirits. The belly of large specimens should be slit to prevent rotting. Details of the specimen, including the date, locality and circumstances of discovery, should be written in soft pencil on a label. It should then be sent to a local museum for identification.

HABITATS OF SOUTHERN AFRICA

This map shows the major vegetation zones in the region. The distributions of many reptiles, particularly lizards, are restricted to specialized habitats within these zones.

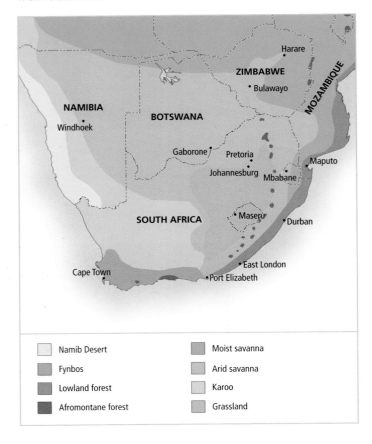

Namib Desert

Fynbos

Lowland forest

Afromontane forest

Moist savanna

Arid savanna

Karoo

Grassland

NAMIB DESERT
This biome is characterized by flat, stony plains, sand dunes and rocky hills and mountains. It is an area of low rainfall with sparse plant growth.

FYNBOS
This biome has a Mediterranean climate with hot, windy summers and cold, wet winters. It is dominated by evergreen shrubby vegetation.

FORESTS
Afromontane forest occurs at higher altitudes and has dense woodland and large trees. Lowland forest occurs at low altitude and has dense, evergreen vegetation with some tall trees.

SAVANNA
This biome is dominated by wooded grassland. Arid savanna is found in the western part of the region. Moist savanna in the northern and eastern parts has higher rainfall.

KAROO
This biome is a low-rainfall semi-desert area with stony plains and low shrubs and succulents. Nama Karoo receives rainfall in summer; in the succulent Karoo, rain falls in winter.

GRASSLAND
This biome occurs at a variety of altitudes. It is a high-rainfall habitat dominated by mixed grassland, with woody plants restricted or absent.

SNAKES Suborder Serpentes

BLIND SNAKES Family Typhlopidae

These primitive snakes have no teeth in the lower jaw. The cylindrical body is covered in small, smooth, overlapping scales, and there are no enlarged belly scales. The vestigial eye consists of a small black spot beneath the head scales. The very short tail ends in a spine. These snakes spend all their life burrowing underground, and feed only on ant eggs and larvae. They are found throughout much of the tropical region, with 8 local species.

DELALANDE'S BEAKED BLIND SNAKE *Rhinotyphlops lalandei* 25–30cm

 This *pink-grey* blind snake can be distinguished by its *slender build* with *26–30 scales at midbody*. A *prominent horizontal edge to the snout* helps it burrow through the ground. It is restricted to the eastern regions of the subcontinent, with scattered records in Namibia. Females lay 2–4 eggs, and the young are flesh-coloured.

BIBRON'S BLIND SNAKE *Afrotyphlops bibronii* 35–40cm

 A stout blind snake, with *30–34 scales around the body* and an *angular snout*. The body is *plain brown*, sometimes olive-brown, with a paler belly. This species is restricted to the highveld and coastal grasslands of South Africa, with a relict population in eastern Zimbabwe. Lays 5–12 thin-walled eggs in summer. The embryos are well-developed at egg laying and take only 5–6 days to hatch.

GIANT BLIND SNAKE *Afrotyphlops mucruso*   60–80cm

This *thick-bodied* blind snake is the largest typhlopid in the world. It is distinguished by having *30–38 scales at midbody* and also has a *prominent horizontal edge to the snout*. Coloration is variable, and the body may be plain or blotched. When the skin is shed the body is *bright blue-grey with dark markings*, but the skin tans with time to a rich red-brown that matches the soil colour. Very large specimens are seen only when forced to the surface by floods. This blind snake lives deep underground, crawling into the brood chambers of ant nests and eating the eggs and larvae. Large fat stores allow it to undertake long fasts. It lays large numbers of eggs (12–40; up to 60 in very large females), which take 5–6 weeks to hatch.

FLOWERPOT SNAKE *Indotyphlops braminus*   14–16cm

A *very small, slender* blind snake that has a *rounded snout, 20 midbody scale rows* and between *300 and 350 scales along the backbone*. It is *uniform grey to pale brown*, with a paler belly and *cream blotches on the snout and anal region*. It is a self-fertilizing, all-female species that lays 2–6 minute (2 x 6mm) eggs. This snake is inadvertently transported in nursery plants, hence its common name. An Asian species, it is now found in numerous countries. It was introduced to Cape Town early in its settlement, and has expanded its range to Durban, as well as Beira in Mozambique.

THREAD SNAKES Family Leptotyphlopidae

These primitive snakes are the smallest in the world. The very thin, cylindrical body is covered in small, smooth scales. Like blind snakes, they lack enlarged belly scales and have vestigial eyes; however, a difference is that they lack teeth in the upper jaw. All local species have blunt heads, and the short tail is relatively longer than that of blind snakes. Thread snakes live underground and follow the chemical trails of ants to their nests. There they eat the eggs, larvae and defenceless workers, swallowing the small prey whole and sucking dry the abdomens of large worker ants. Many species can be distinguished only with the aid of a microscope. Found in Africa, Asia and South America, with 13 local species. Most species lay a small number of elongate eggs that are joined like a string of sausages.

DISTANT'S THREAD SNAKE *Leptotyphlops distanti*   13–20cm

A *thin, grey-black* snake. When dry, the scales may turn silvery in colour and become pale-edged. The *very broad rostral* scale is *fused with the prefrontal*, and is more than half the width of the head, level with the rear border of the eye. The *occipital scales are divided.* This species is almost endemic to South Africa and mainly restricted to moist grasslands in Limpopo and Mpumalanga. It lays a few elongate eggs.

PETER'S THREAD SNAKE *Leptotyphlops scutifrons* complex   18–24cm

These are the most widespread thread snakes in southern Africa, extending from Tanzania to KwaZulu-Natal. They are the most confusing thread snakes, as numerous similar-looking species are involved, many still undescribed. They can be distinguished by the *short tail* (19–39 subcaudal scales) and *wide rostral* (about a third the width of the head at eye level). The tail ends abruptly in a spine. The body is *uniformly black*, but may turn silvery when dry. They are usually found under logs or stones, but may be forced to the surface after heavy rains. Lays 3–7 elongate eggs in summer. When handled, these snakes may turn limp and sham death.

WESTERN THREAD SNAKE *Namibiana occidentalis* 22–32cm

This *very thin* thread snake is the largest local species, and usually has *14 midbody scale rows* and *more than 300 scales along the backbone*. It is *grey-brown to pink-brown* in colour; pale edges to the scales may create a chequered effect. It is mainly restricted to the rocky deserts of Namibia, just extending into the Northern Cape. It may crawl into cracks on rock outcrops, searching for ant nests. This thread snake is likely to be encountered at the surface only on summer nights. Little is known about its reproduction, but it probably lays a few elongate eggs within an ant nest, so that the hatchlings have ready access to food.

LONG-TAILED THREAD SNAKE *Myriopholis longicauda* 18–26cm

A slender thread snake that has *14 midbody scale rows*, but only *10 scales* around the *very long tail* (34–58 subcaudal scales). The *prefrontal scale is separated from the rostral*. The body is *uniformly lilac to dark pink-grey* above, with a fleshy pink belly. It lays 2–4 elongate eggs (4 x 18–22mm).

PYTHONS Family Pythonidae

A diverse family restricted to tropical regions of the Old World. Four species of python are found in Africa, 2 of which occur in southern Africa. Females grow larger, while males have larger spurs alongside the vent. Females hide their eggs in a burrow and guard them. Some Asian species also warm the eggs, either by muscular 'shivering' or by transferring heat from basking.

SOUTHERN AFRICAN PYTHON *Python natalensis*   300–560cm

This is Africa's second largest snake. The *solid, stout body* with very small, smooth scales in *78–95 rows at midbody* make it unmistakable. The triangular head is covered in *small, irregular scales*, and the *upper lips have only 2 heat-sensitive pits* on each side. The body is blotched and *the crown has a large, dark spearhead mark*. This snake favours rocky or bushy areas, usually close to water. They mainly eat small mammals, although large adults may tackle small antelope. Lays up to 100 orange-sized eggs in a hollow tree, termite nest or antbear hole, etc. The female darkens and basks to absorb heat, then coils around her eggs to transfer heat to speed up embryonic development. Although not poisonous, pythons bite readily and can give deep, painful bites. Fatalities are known.

ANCHIETA'S DWARF PYTHON *Python anchietae*   120–180cm

This species can be distinguished from the larger Southern African Python by having only *57–61 rows of scales at midbody*. The triangular *head is also covered with small tubercles*, and the *upper lips have 5 heat-sensitive pits* on each side. The body is pale red-brown, with scattered black-edged, white spots and bands. It lives in the rugged mountains of northern Namibia and Angola, and is a rare and protected species. Small birds, and occasionally rodents, form the main diet. Lays 5 or 6 large eggs in summer. This gentle snake rarely bites, and may roll into a protective ball to hide its head.

AFROMALAGASY SNAKES Family Lamprophiidae

MALAGASY SNAKES Subfamily Pseudoxyrhophiinae

The majority of the 90 snakes in this subfamily are restricted to Madagascar, with a few reaching other Indian Ocean islands. Three genera, each with just one or a few species, occur in the eastern regions of sub-Saharan Africa.

COMMON SLUG-EATER *Duberria lutrix*   30–43cm

This shy, *stout-bodied* little snake has a small head. It has *15 midbody scale rows*, and *few (116–142) ventral scales*. The back is *brick red to pale brown*, sometimes with a *broken black line along the backbone*. The paler flanks vary from grey to pale brown, and the belly is *cream, edged with a dark dotted line.* It is a gardener's friend, as it feeds entirely on slugs and snails, which it finds by following their slime trails. It is usually found hiding in damp locations, such as grass roots, rotting logs, or compost heaps, but may move around on humid, overcast days. Gives birth to 6–9 young in late summer. When handled, this snake may roll into a tight spiral (hence the Afrikaans name 'tabakrolletjie') and release an unpleasant cloacal fluid.

VARIEGATED SLUG-EATER *Duberria variegata*   30–40cm

Similar in habits and appearance to the Common Slug-eater, this snake has a more prominent snout and even fewer *ventral scales (91–110).* The *brick-red, olive-brown or dark brown back* also has *3 rows of blackish spots* that may fuse to form irregular crossbars. The dirty yellow belly has dark reticulations,

particularly towards the rear. This species is restricted to coastal dune vegetation in northern Zululand and adjacent Mozambique. It feeds exclusively on slugs and snails. Gives birth to 7–20 young in late summer. Although it may wriggle in the hand, it does not form a spiral, but often discharges an unpleasant cloacal fluid.

MANY-SPOTTED SNAKE *Amplorhinus multimaculatus* 45–60cm

Luke Verbrugt

This unusual, secretive snake is found in isolated populations in the cool, moist eastern regions. The small head has moderate-sized *eyes with round pupils*, and there are *17 midbody scale rows* and a *longish tail*. Coloration is variable. The body may vary from leaf green to olive-brown, usually with a series of dark blotches and sometimes with a pale dorsolateral stripe. Scattered, pale-edged scales may give a flecked appearance. It has *grooved back fangs*, and catches frogs in the early evening in reedbeds and waterside vegetation. Gives birth to 4–12 young in late summer. This snake's venom is considered harmless.

MOLE SNAKES Family Pseudaspinae

A very small subfamily containing just 2 snakes: the first species is almost endemic to the subcontinent, the other is one of Africa's iconic and widespread snakes.

WESTERN KEELED SNAKE *Pythonodipsas carinatus* 45–60cm

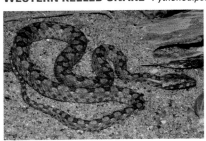

Superficially viper-like, this rare, nocturnal snake is easily recognized by its *long, thin body* and *fragmented head scales*. The *flat head* has a distinct neck and *large eyes with vertical pupils*. The *swollen nostrils are situated on top of the snout*. The back has various pastel colours, and a *double series of dark-edged blotches* that may fuse into a zigzag or irregular crossbars. This species is found in rocky desert, where it feeds on small lizards and rodents. Females grow much larger than males, which seldom exceed 40cm. This snake is believed to be oviparous.

MOLE SNAKE *Pseudaspis cana*

100–160cm

A widespread *large* snake, easily recognized by its *thick body, slightly hooked snout*, and *small eyes with round pupils*. The body scales are usually smooth, but sometimes keeled in black snakes from the southwestern Cape, where it may also grow to 2m. Colour varies with region and age. Young are always *pale brown with 4 rows of dark, pale-edged spots*. These usually fade in subadults (about 1m), but may persist in some adults. Adults are uniform pale to red-brown, sometimes grey-olive to dark brown, and usually jet black in the southwestern Cape. It is a useful constrictor that lives underground, hunting rodents, particularly large molerats. Gives birth to a large litter, of up to 95 young, in late summer. Adult males often fight, inflicting deep cuts on each other with their numerous teeth. Mole Snakes are not poisonous, but can give a deep and painful bite.

SHOVEL-SNOUTED SNAKES Subfamily Prosymninae

Another endemic African subfamily, containing a single genus of 16 species. Found through the savannas and woodlands of sub-Saharan Africa. Shovel-snouted snakes are easily distinguished by the *angular edge to the snout*. This 'shovel' aids the search in soft soils for reptile eggs, which form the sole diet. When a clutch of reptile eggs is found, the eggs are either swallowed whole, or are slit and the liquid yolk drunk. Fat stores allow these snakes to survive long fasts between breeding seasons.

SUNDEVALL'S SHOVEL-SNOUT *Prosymna sundevallii*

24–36cm

A small species with the 'shovel' *upturned*. The body is cylindrical with *smooth scales*. The short *tail ends in a spine*. Individuals in the southern and central regions have a *paired row of dark spots* on the pale to dark brown body, whereas those found in the northern and eastern regions have a *single row*. The belly is white. This snake lays a small clutch of 3–5 elongate eggs in summer.

TWO-STRIPED SHOVEL-SNOUT *Prosymna bivittata* 26–35cm

 Although very similar in appearance to Sundevall's Shovel-snout, this species can be distinguished by the prominent *broken orange stripe that runs along the backbone*. The rest of the body is purple-brown and the belly is white. This snake is usually found under stones or rotting trees on sandy soil in the arid savanna of the Kalahari region. There is an isolated population along the lower Orange River. Lays up to 4 elongate eggs in summer.

SOUTH-WESTERN SHOVEL-SNOUT *Prosymna frontalis* 30–44cm

 The longest and thinnest shovel-snout in the region. The angular snout is *not upturned* and the *fused internasals form a single band* behind the snout. The relatively *long tail has 32–54 subcaudal scales.*

 The body is pale brown to chestnut above, and a dark edge to each scale creates a striped or stippled effect. A *broad, dark brown collar* covers the neck and fainter crossbars may occur on the forebody, particularly in juveniles. The belly is white. This snake inhabits the western arid regions, where it is usually found under stones on sandy soil, or crossing tracks at night after rain. Little is known of its reproduction.

EAST AFRICAN SHOVEL-SNOUT *Prosymna stuhlmannii* 24–28cm

A small snake with a *rounded snout and 2 postocular scales*. The short tail has only *17–39 subcaudal scales*. The dorsal scales have a single apical pit and are in *17 midbody rows*. The dark brown to metallic blue-black body usually has *pale-centred scales*, and *paired small white spots may flank the*

backbone. The belly is usually white, but may be brown-black. The snout is usually infused with yellow. This snake is found in wooded savanna in the southern regions. Like all shovel-snouts, it eats only reptile eggs. It lays 3 or 4 elongate eggs in leaf litter in the rainy season. Shy and secretive, it never bites or wriggles violently.

HOUSE SNAKES AND RELATIVES Subfamily Lamprophiinae

Restricted to Africa, these are characteristically nocturnal snakes, which lack fangs and kill by constriction. They are harmless, usually terrestrial, and lay eggs.

COMMON BROWN WATER SNAKE
Lycodonomorphus rufulus 60–85cm

This gentle, inoffensive species is the commonest water snake in southern Africa. The eyes have *elliptical pupils* and are *set on the sides of the small head*. The *first upper labial lacks a backward projection*. The plain olive body has smooth scales in *19 rows at midbody. The upper lip is not spotted and, like the belly, is pale yellow-pink in colour*. In many individuals the *longish tail (53–86 subcaudal scales)* is darker below. This snake hunts at night, and is frequently found under cover around water margins. Small frogs form the main prey and are constricted. Lays 6–10 eggs in late summer.

DUSKY-BELLIED WATER SNAKE
Lycodonomorphus laevissimus

70–120cm

Johan Marais

This is the largest water snake in the region. The small eyes have *round pupils* and are set high on the *sides of the small, flattened head*. The *scales at midbody are in 19 rows*. The *first upper labial has an obvious backward projection*. The back is *uniform olive to brown-black*, sometimes with a pale stripe on the lower flank. The belly is cream to yellow, with a *broad central dark band*. The *upper lip is usually spotted*. A very aquatic species, often found submerged in quiet backwaters and pools, where it searches for prey during the day among rocks and sunken logs. Tadpoles, frogs and fish form its main diet. Lays up to 17 eggs in summer. Bad-tempered and ever ready to bite, this snake may also void a foul-smelling cloacal fluid when annoyed.

FLOODPLAIN WATER SNAKE
Lycodonomorphus obscuriventris

50–66cm

André Coetzer

A rare East African species, extending south along the Mozambique floodplain as far as northern KwaZulu-Natal. It is a small snake, easily confused with the Common Brown Water Snake. However, the body is *dark olive to blackish* and the *upper lip has a prominent yellow stripe*. The *orange-yellow belly is sometimes faintly spotted*. The short tail (*37–52 subcaudal scales*) is dark below. This snake is secretive and hunts for frogs and tadpoles in the late afternoon or early evening. A gentle, shy species that is most likely to be encountered foraging in the wet margins of small vleis and streams. There are no breeding records.

OLIVE SNAKE *Lycodonomorphus inornatus* 60–130cm

Werner Conradie

A large, thick-bodied snake previously confused with house snakes. Restricted to the moister coastal regions of the southern Cape and KwaZulu-Natal, extending along the eastern

escarpment. It is *uniform olive-green* in colour (often blacker in the north), with a pale grey-green belly. Unlike other olive-coloured water snakes, it has *21–25 midbody scale rows* and *no patterning on the belly or beneath the tail*. This snake is terrestrial, and rodents form the main diet, although it also eats frogs and even other snakes. Lays 5–15 eggs in summer. This snake usually has a peaceful disposition and settles well into captivity.

BROWN HOUSE SNAKE *Boaedon capensis* complex 60–150cm

These large house snakes were thought to be one species for many years, but are now known to comprise numerous cryptic species. They occur throughout the region, and usually have

a *rust-red body*, off-white belly and a pair of *thin yellow-white stripes on the side of the head and neck*. The *head is triangular, with large eyes with vertical pupils*. Some western populations are paler and have larger eyes (*mentalis* phase). Individuals from KwaZulu-Natal often have stripes that continue along the body. All species are terrestrial and nocturnal, and feed mainly on rodents, such as mice and rats, although juveniles also eat lizards. They are tolerant of urban squalor, occurring commonly around houses (hence their common name), where they help control rodent pests. Lays up to 18 elongate eggs (12–24 x 25–56mm) in summer, and the young measure up to 26cm. They are harmless and kill their prey by constriction.

AURORA HOUSE SNAKE *Lamprophis aurora* 50–90cm

This pretty, gentle house snake is rare. It is of similar coloration and distribution to the Olive Snake but can be distinguished by the *prominent orange-yellow stripe along the backbone*. The young sparkle, each scale having a *pale yellow bar*. This imparts a speckled appearance, which

could cause confusion with the spotted phase of the Harlequin Snake. However, this species lacks front fangs and is completely harmless. Nocturnal, it feeds mainly on nestling rodents, although lizards and frogs are also eaten. Lays 8–12 eggs, and the hatchlings are about 20cm long.

SPOTTED HOUSE SNAKE *Lamprophis guttatus* 40–62cm

Although rarely seen, this small, slender house snake is common in rock outcrops of the Karoo and eastern escarpment mountains. The *head is flattened, with large eyes*. Coloration is varied, but the *body is always blotched*. In the Western Cape the body is pale brown or tan with alternating or paired dark brown blotches on the forebody. In KwaZulu-

Natal and Mpumalanga the body is pinkish to silvery-grey with large, pale-edged, purple-brown blotches that extend along the whole body and may fuse to form a zigzag pattern. It is a shy species that shelters in rock cracks during the day and hunts at night for lizards. Lays up to 8 eggs in summer.

FISK'S HOUSE SNAKE *Lamprophis fiskii* 25–35cm

Few local snakes are as beautiful, or as rare, as this diminutive house snake. The *lemon yellow body* has a *double row of alternating dark brown blotches*, that may fuse to form a zigzag pattern. The belly is creamy white. The rounded head has *large eyes, with vertical pupils*, while the *tail is relatively short* (28–34 subcaudals). Fewer than 40 specimens are known, from widely scattered localities in the Karoo and Little Namaqualand, Northern Cape. This snake probably spends much of its time underground, emerging at night to feed on lizards. When annoyed, it hisses and tightly coils and uncoils the front and rear of its body in a similar behaviour to that of some shovel-snout snakes. There are no breeding records.

YELLOW-BELLIED HOUSE SNAKE *Lamprophis fuscus* 45–76cm

Few people have seen this species, although it is widely distributed in the eastern regions. It is a *slender, rounded-headed* house snake, with a *relatively long tail* (56–74 subcaudal scales). The back is *plain and dark to pale olive*, while characteristically the *belly, flanks and upper lip are bright yellow*. There are only *19 midbody scale rows*. This snake spends most of its life underground, particularly in old termite nests, where it feeds on nestling rodents. It may also eat small geckos that use termite nests as retreats. Lays a small clutch of elongate eggs in summer. This snake has a gentle disposition, but does not settle well into captivity.

CAPE WOLF SNAKE *Lycophidion capense* 35–64cm

Wolf snakes are peculiar to Africa. They are named after their long, recurved teeth; however, they are harmless, gentle snakes. This common species is found all the way from the Cape to Somalia. It is a small snake, with a *flattened head* that is hardly distinct from the body. The *eyes are small with vertical pupils*, and the *first upper labial contacts the postnasal*. The body is *uniform grey-black* (browner in the southern regions), often with *each scale white-tipped*. This snake shelters by day, emerging at dusk to search for prey. The diet consists mainly of diurnal lizards such as skinks and sand lizards, which are caught sleeping in their retreats. Lays 3–8 eggs in summer.

PYGMY WOLF SNAKE *Lycophidion pygmaeum* 20–30cm

A small snake restricted to the eastern coastal regions. It is a rare, terrestrial species, sheltering in grass tussocks in coastal grasslands. The *grey-blue to purple-brown body* appears faintly speckled due to the pale-edged scales. There is a characteristic *pale edge to the blunt head*, from the snout to the temporal region. The *dark belly has pale-edged ventral scales*. The diet consists of small burrowing skinks. One large female collected was carrying 3 eggs. **NT**

NAMIBIAN WOLF SNAKE *Lycophidion namibianum* 35–59cm

Although easily confused with the Cape Wolf Snake, this species differs in having *a reddish to dark brown back*, scales *heavily speckled with white*, and a *broad white band on the lower flanks*. There is also usually a dark brown stripe along the middle of the belly. *The first upper labial is separated from the postnasal.* This species has mostly been collected from rocky areas in bushy scrubland in northern Namibia and adjacent Angola. Nothing is known of its diet or reproduction, although these are likely to be similar to those of other wolf snakes.

SWAZI ROCK SNAKE *Inyoka swazicus* 60–90cm

An unusual snake, with a *long, slender body*, and a distinct, *flattened head with large, bulging eyes*. There are only *17 midbody scale rows*. The body is *uniform pale to dark red-brown* with a creamy white belly. This species is endemic to the eastern Mpumalanga mountains and western Swaziland, where it inhabits rock outcrops. It is usually found sheltering during the day under rock flakes. It hunts at night, when its large eyes with vertical pupils help it to find sleeping lizards. Lays a small number (up to 7) of elongate eggs in summer.

SOUTHERN FILE SNAKE *Gonionotophis capensis* 100–175cm

An unusual and rarely seen snake, easily recognized by its *thickset triangular body* and *very flat head*. The almost *conical, strongly keeled scales* are *separated by bare, pink-purple skin*, and the *scales along the backbone are white, enlarged*

and have 2 keels. The body is grey-brown with ivory-cream belly and flanks. This species is a formidable predator of other snakes, which it kills by constriction. It will even tackle venomous snakes, including cobras, to whose venom it is immune. Females grow larger than males, and a clutch of 5–13 relatively large eggs are laid in leaf litter in summer. Docile in disposition, it never bites. Its only offensive behaviour is to void its bowels when handled.

BLACK FILE SNAKE *Gonionotophis nyassae* 40–65cm

The *flattened head, triangular body* and *pinkish skin between the body scales* confirm this is a file snake. It can be distinguished from Southern File Snake by its *uniform purple-black colour*, although the belly may be creamy white.

In addition, it has a *slightly longer tail* (51–77 subcaudal scales) and *fewer ventral scales* (fewer than 190). It inhabits mainly savanna, but may enter coastal forest. The diet consists mainly of lizards, particularly skinks, but this species will take small snakes. Lays up to 6 eggs in summer. This small, shy snake rarely bites and usually moves jerkily in the hand, trying to hide its head under body coils.

SAND SNAKES AND RELATIVES Subfamily Psammophiinae

Sand and Whip snakes occur mainly in Africa, with a few species
in Eurasia and Madagascar. They are diurnal and mainly terrestrial,
possessing enlarged back fangs and they kill by injecting venom.
The bites of only a few species are of clinical importance.

RHOMBIC SKAAPSTEKER *Psammophylax rhombeatus*   80–140cm

The unusual
common name
of this snake is
unjustified. Its bite
is less dangerous
than a bee sting and
certainly less painful.
The *smallish head*
has a *rounded snout*,
there are *17 midbody
scale rows*, and the
tail is moderately
long with 60–84
subcaudal scales.

The *yellowish-brown back has 3 or 4 rows of dark-edged blotches*,
that may fuse to form an irregular zigzag pattern or stripes
(particularly in KwaZulu-Natal and Wild Coast). This snake hunts
during the day in moist grasslands, and feeds on a wide variety
of prey, including mice, frogs and lizards. Lays up to 30 eggs in a
hole, and the female is often found coiled around them.

STRIPED SKAAPSTEKER *Psammophylax tritaeniatus*   60–93cm

Johan Marais

Slightly smaller,
but similar in
build to Rhombic
Skaapsteker, this
attractive snake
can be distinguished by its more
pointed snout and *shorter tail*
(49–69 subcaudal scales). It has a
prominent striped pattern, with
3 black-edged dark brown stripes
on a pale grey body. The middle
stripe may be divided by a fine
yellow line. The upper lip and belly are plain white. This snake hunts small
mice in the northern savannas, but will also take frogs and lizards. Lays up to
18 eggs in a hole in summer, but are not guarded by the female. Gentle and
inoffensive, this species may wriggle in the hand, but never bites.

OLIVE GRASS SNAKE *Psammophis mossambicus* 120–180cm

This is a big, *robust* snake, with a *long tail* and large scales in *17 midbody rows*. There are usually *more than 164 ventral scales*. The *olive-brown back* is paler towards the tail, and may have scattered black flecks on the sides of the forebody. Sometimes the

body scales are black-edged to form thin black stripes. The white-yellow belly may have black streaks. This snake is an active, diurnal hunter that often moves with the forebody lifted. It eats various small vertebrates, including other snakes, and is a nervous snake that swiftly retreats into cover, but will bite readily when caught. It lays 10–30 eggs in midsummer. The mild venom may cause nausea, local swelling and pain, but it is not dangerous.

SHORT-SNOUTED GRASS SNAKE
Psammophis brevirostris 90–120cm

Easily confused with the Olive Grass Snake, as it is similar in appearance and habits. However, this species is smaller, *more slender* and usually has *fewer than 164 ventral scales*. The pattern is *often striped*, usually

with a *white 'stitch line' down the backbone* and a paler band on the flanks. The belly is white or yellow, often with a black spotted line on each side. This snake has a relatively short snout, hence its common and scientific names. It prefers dry grassland and savanna, where it hunts small vertebrates, particularly mice and lizards. Lays 4–15 eggs in summer.

Johan Marais

WESTERN STRIPE-BELLIED SAND SNAKE
Psammophis subtaeniatus   90–130cm

A beautiful, *slender* snake, but one that rarely stops to be enjoyed. The *bright yellow belly, bordered by black and white stripes*, is unmistakable. The back is also striped, with a *broad, black-edged dorsal band flanked by cream and brown*

stripes. This snake is often seen moving with its head up, alert for prey, and may also climb into low bushes. It is a fast, active hunter of birds, lizards and mice in the open savannas of the northern regions. Due to its speed and alertness, it is difficult to catch, although many are caught by birds of prey. Lays 4–10 elongate eggs in an underground tunnel.

WESTERN SAND SNAKE *Psammophis trigrammus*   90–120cm

The *most slender* sand snake in the region. The *very long tail is more than half the body length* and has 132–155 subcaudal scales. Body colour is cryptic *olive to grey-brown*, often with a *reddish-brown dorsal stripe* and yellowish-white lateral stripe. The off-white belly may have a grey to olive band down the middle. This snake is restricted to sparse bush in the western arid regions, but avoids open dune areas. It hunts sand lizards and skinks during the heat of the day, pursuing them speedily and grabbing them before they can escape into cover. Prey is not constricted, but simply swallowed alive. Like other sand snakes, it lays a small clutch of elongate eggs underground.

NAMIB SAND SNAKE *Psammophis namibensis* 100–140cm

 A brightly coloured, boldly striped snake with a *dark dorsal band* that is often broken with a *conspicuous thin, dashed line down the spine* and a bold *reddish-orange lateral stripe*. The *top of the head is spotted or barred*. The *anal scale is divided*. Like other sand snakes, it often forages with the head held up, alert for movement. It chases small lizards, which are seized and swallowed alive. Lays 4–9 elongate eggs in summer.

KAROO SAND SNAKE *Psammophis notostictus* 80–110cm

 Very similar to the Namib Sand Snake, but usually *duller in coloration*. In the hand, it can be distinguished by having an *undivided anal scale*. It is one of the commonest snakes of the Karoo and adjacent regions, and is often seen sunning itself on roads during the heat of the day. It is very difficult to catch as it is capable of moving very quickly. Lizards form the main diet and are caught after a speedy chase. They are quickly subdued by the mild venom and are swallowed head first. At night this snake shelters in a rock crack or rodent burrow. Lays a small clutch of 3–8 elongate eggs in summer.

DWARF SAND SNAKE *Psammophis angolensis* 30–50 cm

This elegant, tiny sand snake is rarely seen. It has *11 scale rows at midbody* and a *conspicuously striped body*, with a *broad brown-black dorsal stripe* and a faint broken black stripe on the lower flank. The *dark brown head has 3 narrow crossbars* and 1 or several dark neck collars. This snake forages among grass tussocks and fallen logs in the lowveld savanna, where it feeds on small lizards and frogs. It is a shy, gentle species that seldom bites, but unfortunately does not settle well into captivity. The female lays a small clutch of 3–5 elongate eggs in moist soil under a log.

CROSS-MARKED GRASS SNAKE *Psammophis crucifer* 50–82 cm

A temperate species, restricted to cool, moist fynbos in the southern Cape coastal regions, with scattered populations in montane grassland in the northeast and along the West Coast to the Richtersveld. Small and robust, and the *tail is relatively shorter* than that of other sand snakes (61–81 subcaudal scales).

The *silver-grey back* usually has a *broad, black-edged, brown dorsal stripe*, with a similar stripe on the flanks. The head has *dark-edged, cream-yellow crossbars*. Occasional specimens lack stripes and are plain grey-olive in colour. Lizards and frogs form the main diet, and 5–13 eggs are laid in midsummer.

DWARF BEAKED SNAKE *Dipsina multimaculata* 30–50cm

This small, slender snake comes in a wide variety of ground colours that closely match that of the sand in the western rocky deserts. Has *3–5 rows of dark, sometimes pale-centred, blotches on the back*, which may fuse to form irregular crossbars. The *neck has a dark V-shape*, and the distinct head has a *prominent hooked snout*. The *short tail has only 28–45 paired subcaudal scales*. This cryptic, slow-moving snake ambushes small lizards from its hiding place in loose sand at the base of a bush or stone. When threatened, it may coil and hiss, pretending to be a small adder. Nonetheless, it is harmless.

RUFOUS BEAKED SNAKE *Rhamphiophis rostratus* 120–160cm

Like the Dwarf Beaked Snake, it is characterized by a *prominent hooked snout*. However, it is a *much larger, stout-bodied* snake, and the *long tail has 87–118 paired subcaudal scales*. The body is spotted in juveniles, but a *uniform red-tan colour* in adults, sometimes with *pale-*

centred scales. The head has a distinctive *dark brown eye stripe*. This snake shelters in a burrow in the northern sandy bushveld, and eats a variety of small vertebrates, including other snakes. It may hiss and strike when first caught, but tames well. Lays 8–17 large eggs, often staggered over several days.

BARK SNAKE *Hemirhagerrhis nototaenia* 25–40cm

A pretty, but secretive snake that shelters under loose bark or in hollow trees in the northern savannas. It is *small and slender*, with a distinct, *flattened head and large eyes with vertical pupils*. The grey back has a *dark dorsal stripe* often fused with a series of black spots on the flanks. The

tail is dirty orange and the *belly is heavily stippled in grey-brown.* This species feeds mainly on small lizards, particularly dwarf day geckos, although it may also eat small tree frogs. The snake swallows its food while hanging head down in the branches. Lays a small clutch of 2–8 elongate eggs in a tree hollow.

WESTERN ROCK SNAKE *Hemirhagerrhis viperina* 25–40cm

A vividly patterned, secretive snake that shelters under loose flakes on rock outcrops in northern Namibia and Angola. It has a distinct, *flattened head and large eyes with vertical pupils*. The back is *cream to pale orange* with a *conspicuous dark zigzag stripe* that may have rust-red patches. The *tail is often bright orange* and the *belly is cream, sometimes with pale grey stippling.* This snake is often found basking on sun-warmed rocks. Its main diet consists of small lizards, particularly skinks and day geckos. Nothing is known of its reproduction.

AFRICAN BURROWING SNAKES Subfamily Atractaspidinae

These snakes are peculiar to Africa. Most are back-fanged (absent in 1 species), while burrowing asps have evolved partially erectile front fangs and a unique venom. They push through loose soil or sand, hunting mainly other burrowing reptiles.

BICOLOURED QUILL-SNOUTED SNAKE
Xenocalamus bicolor   45–72cm

Quill-snouted snakes are so bizarre they cannot be confused with any other snakes. They have a *thin, very elongate body* and a *quill-shaped head with underslung mouth.* The *minute eyes have round pupils,* and the *tail is short and blunt,* ending in a *spine.* Coloration

in this species is very varied, and may be striped, spotted or mottled, and even all black. It is found in scattered populations in the sandy western and northern bushveld. It burrows in deep sand searching for worm lizards, which form its exclusive diet. Lays 3 or 4 elongate eggs in summer.

TRANSVAAL QUILL-SNOUTED SNAKE
Xenocalamus transvaalensis   30–47cm

This small snake has a *thin body* and a *quill-shaped head* with an *underslung mouth.* The body is yellow with black-centred dorsal scales that give a *chequered appearance.* This species is found in 2 isolated populations in the eastern lowlands, where it burrows in shallow sand searching for worm lizards. Lays 2 or 3 very elongate eggs (6 x 28mm) in summer.

CAPE CENTIPEDE-EATER *Aparallactus capensis* 25–35cm

Although very common in grassland and savanna, this small, slender snake is rarely seen. It has a *small head*, with a *rounded snout* and a *prominent black collar*. The body varies in colour from *red-brown to grey-buff*, with a cream belly. This snake spends most of its life underground, in tunnels, rotting logs or rock piles, and particularly old termite nests. It hunts centipedes, which form its sole diet. Although some centipedes are large and have venom claws, they are fearlessly seized and quickly succumb to the snake's venom, which is completely harmless to humans. Lays 2–4 small, elongate eggs in summer.

PLUMBEOUS/RETICULATED CENTIPEDE-EATER
Aparallactus lunulatus 35–54cm

This East African species extends south to Zimbabwe and through the lowveld to Swaziland, where it inhabits sandy soils in moist savanna. It is similar in build and habits to the Cape Centipede-eater. There are 2 colour forms; the first has an *unpatterned blue-grey head and body*, the other a *brown body* with *black-edged scales* and a *series of vague darker blotches along the spine*. In addition to centipedes, this species also hunts scorpions under logs and stones in patches of moist evergreen forest. Lays 3 or 4 elongate eggs (7 x 30mm) in summer.

COMMON PURPLE-GLOSSED SNAKE
Amblyodipsas polylepis

50–110cm

This *black snake* has smooth scales that have an attractive purple gloss when freshly shed. Unlike the Natal Black Snake (opposite), with which it is easily confused, it has *15–31 paired subcaudal scales*. It is a *stocky* snake, with a *blunt head and small eyes*. There are *19–21*

midbody scale rows, and usually *only 6 upper labials*. It is a gentle snake and rarely bites. This species is found in the moister regions of the northeastern savannas, and feeds mainly on other burrowing reptiles, particularly blind snakes. It swallows small prey alive, while larger prey is subdued by constriction, often after lengthy battles. Lays up to 10 relatively large eggs.

SMALL-EYED PURPLE-GLOSSED SNAKE
Amblyodipsas microphthalma

25–33cm

A small, smooth-scaled snake of sandy soils in the northern lowveld and northeastern KwaZulu-Natal. The small head has a *slightly pointed snout and small eyes*. The body may be uniform glossy black (in the north) or blue-black backed, with bright yellow on the lower flanks and belly (in the south). It has only *15 midbody scale rows* and *18–26 paired subcaudal scales*. This snake burrows in loose sandy litter, hunting legless skinks and small worm lizards. Reproduction is unknown, but it probably lays a few elongate eggs.

NATAL BLACK SNAKE *Macrelaps microlepidotus* 70–120cm

Like the Common Purple-glossed Snake (opposite), this *burrowing, shiny black snake* feeds on other burrowing reptiles, although it also readily takes small mice and frogs. It lacks erectile fangs, but still has a toxic venom that has caused nausea but no deaths. This species

can be distinguished by its *larger size* and *fatter body*. It also has *no terminal spine on the tail*. This snake is endemic to the eastern coastal regions of South Africa, where it can be found burrowing in deep leaf litter in coastal bush, from Stutterheim to Zululand. It lays a relatively large clutch of up to 18 eggs. **NT**

SOUTHERN/BIBRON'S BURROWING ASP
Atractaspis bibronii 40–70cm

The *long, erectile front fangs* of this snake could cause confusion with vipers, with which they were long classified (as mole vipers). Many individuals are all black, above and beneath, whilst others have a prominent white belly. The short tail has *undivided subcaudal scales* and a *terminal spine*. It is usually found sheltering in rock piles, in old termitaria, or under rotting logs, where it searches for other burrowing reptiles. It may also eat nestling mice. Although the venom of this unusual snake is very painful, it has caused no known deaths. Nonetheless, it bites readily and is best left well alone, and *cannot be safely held behind the neck*. It lays a small clutch of up to 6 elongate eggs.

SPOTTED HARLEQUIN SNAKE ☠ *Homoroselaps lacteus* 35–65cm

Unmistakable due to its bright colours, this *small, slender snake* is the region's most beautiful species. It is found in a number of different colour phases. In the south and west it is patterned in *black and yellow*, with a *bright red dorsal stripe* that may be broken into spots. From East London northwards it is *all black with a yellow dot on each scale*, and a *yellow dorsal stripe*. This snake is found under stones or rotting logs on sandy soil, and feeds mainly on other snakes and legless lizards. It lays 6–16 small, elongate eggs. This snake's bite is painful, causing swelling, bruising and painful lymph glands, but is not fatal.

STRIPED HARLEQUIN SNAKE *Homoroselaps dorsalis* 20–32cm

Johan Marais

This minute, but elegant snake is easily recognized by its *very slender body*, which is *black with a lemon-yellow dorsal stripe*. The lips, flanks and belly are yellow-white. This snake lives underground, particularly in old termite nests in the grasslands of southern Mpumalanga and the adjacent KwaZulu-Natal and Free State. It is relatively rare and very little is known of its biology. It lays 2–4 small, elongate eggs. **NT**

OLD WORLD WATER SNAKES Family Natricidae

Distributed mainly throughout the northern hemisphere, with few African representatives (11 species in 4 genera). These snakes usually lack fangs and kill by constriction. Most species are diurnal and of aquatic or semi-aquatic habits. All African species are harmless.

FOREST MARSH SNAKE *Natriciteres sylvatica* 30–46cm

This is a *small snake* with *smooth scales* in *17 rows at midbody*. The *tail is relatively long* (60–84 subcaudal scales) and may be shed if grabbed, although it cannot be regenerated. The body is *dark olive to blackish*, often with a *row of white dots down the backbone*. A *faint yellow collar* may be present on the neck, and the *belly is yellow-orange*. This species is found in wet montane and lowland forest, and occurs in isolated populations in northern Zululand and eastern Zimbabwe. It frequents dead logs and rotting vegetation at forest fringes, where it usually hunts frogs. It may even eat large, fish-eating spiders. This snake lays up to 6 eggs in moist leaf litter in summer.

STRIPED SWAMP SNAKE *Limnophis bangweolicus* 45–63cm

A small, inconspicuous snake with a *cylindrical body and small head*. It can be distinguished from the marsh snakes by having a *single, triangular internasal scale on top of the snout*. The largish eyes have *round pupils*. The body has a striped appearance due to *3 or 4 black-edged scale rows on the flanks*. The bright *belly is yellow to brick red*. Shy and secretive, this snake hunts small frogs and possibly small fish in the marshes of the Okavango and Zambezi River valleys. Little is known of its reproduction; a large female collected contained 5 eggs.

RACERS AND RELATIVES Family Colubridae

The group includes many of the typical snakes of the northern hemisphere. It is well represented in Africa, with many groups lacking fangs, and others back-fanged, with some highly venomous.

COMMON EGG-EATER *Dasypeltis scabra*   55–90cm

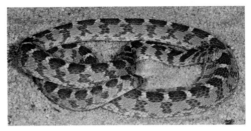

Found throughout southern Africa, this *thin-bodied grey snake* has *numerous dark blotches* along the body and a *prominent dark V-shape* mark on the neck. It has *strongly keeled body scales,* which are *oblique*

on the lower flanks. These scales cause a hissing sound when rubbed against each other. This sound and the snake's coloration mimic some small adders. Egg-eaters have adapted to a strict diet of bird's eggs. The eggs are swallowed whole, and special throat 'teeth' (projections into the gullet from the backbone) saw through the eggshell. The liquid content is then swallowed, and the collapsed eggshell is regurgitated. When disturbed, an egg-eater puts on a great pretence of being dangerous. It gapes its mouth wide, *revealing a black lining*, and strikes readily. It is a dramatic display, but this snake is almost toothless, and completely harmless. These snakes are prolific breeders, laying up to 25 eggs.

EAST COAST EGG-EATER *Dasypeltis medici*   60–90cm

A secretive, beautiful egg-eater with a small head, largish eyes, round pupils, and *strongly keeled body scales*. The body is a warm pink or pinkish-grey, with a *dark stripe along the backbone,* interrupted by *small white bars that extend*

as narrow dark bars onto the pale flanks. Has *3–7 narrow V-shapes on the neck*. The *mouth lining is pinkish*. This is an arboreal species, restricted to coastal and riverine forest. Lays 6–28 eggs. This species is harmless.

KUNENE RACER *Hemerophis zebrinus*   40–66cm

This snake's elongate body has *smooth scales* in 23 rows at midbody. The *tail is relatively long* and the *anal shield is divided*. The *greyish body has numerous irregular dark crossbars* that fade towards the tail. The *head has a dark bar on the side*, and the snout and lips are yellowish. A very rare snake, known from only 3 specimens, one of which escaped! It is restricted to northern Namibia, but may extend into adjacent Angola. Nothing is known of its biology. A close relative, Smith's Racer of East Africa, is terrestrial, diurnal, and chases down small lizards. Kunene Racer is easily confused with a juvenile Zebra Cobra (p.53), but is unlikely to be venomous.

MARBLED TREE SNAKE *Dipsadoboa aulica*   50–85cm

This snake's *big head is finely marbled with white*, and the *large eyes have vertical pupils*. The pale brown back has *38–57 pale, dark-edged crossbars* in juveniles. These decrease in size and number with growth. A rare, secretive inhabitant of mature forest along the large rivers of the eastern lowveld and adjacent Mozambique and Zimbabwe. During the day it shelters in bamboo and palm thicket, emerging at night to feed on geckos and reed frogs. When first caught it is very willing to bite, adopting an open coiled posture. This snake lays eggs, but little else is known about its breeding.

EASTERN TIGER SNAKE   *Telescopus semiannulatus*   60–100cm

This distinctive, nocturnal species is thin-bodied, with an obvious *flat head and large eyes*. It has *19 midbody scale rows* and a *divided anal shield*. The dull orange body bears *22–50 dark blotches,* which are larger on the forebody. Although mainly terrestrial, and often found crossing roads on wet summer nights, it regularly climbs into trees or house roofs to search for food. It mainly feeds on small birds and lizards, although also catches mice and bats. When disturbed, these snakes will bite readily and often, but their venom is not dangerous. Lays 6–20 eggs in moist leaf litter.

NAMIB TIGER SNAKE   *Telescopus beetzi*   40–68cm

Similar in appearance to Eastern Tiger Snake, but with a *sandy-buff coloration* and more *dark blotches (30–39 on the body and 12–20 on the tail)*. It also has *21 midbody scale rows* and an *undivided anal shield*. This species is shy, sheltering in rock outcrops in the western deserts and scrublands. This snake is nocturnal, emerging at night to hunt lizards. Smaller and less aggressive than the Eastern Tiger Snake, it lays a small clutch of 3–6 eggs in summer.

SPOTTED BUSH SNAKE *Philothamnus semivariegatus* 80–120cm

A beautiful, diurnal snake that hunts among bushes on rocky ridges or along river courses. The *slender body* has a *long tail*. A *lateral keel runs* on each side of the belly and tail. The green body has *black spots or crossbars* on the forepart and may become grey-bronze towards the tail. This snake is an expert and speedy climber, and pursues lizards and tree frogs. When confronted, it inflates the throat to expose *vivid blue skin between the scales* and strikes readily, but despite this bluff it is harmless. Lays a small clutch of 3–12 eggs in midsummer.

WESTERN GREEN SNAKE *Philothamnus angolensis* 80–115cm

More robust than Spotted Bush Snake and usually found hunting in reedbeds and vegetation along major river courses. The body is a *bright emerald green*, without black spots but with scattered *bluish-white scales*. This

snake feeds on frogs and lizards, but will also take nestling weaver birds. Like the Spotted Bush Snake, it inflates its throat when threatened, but has *black skin between the scales*. Lays up to 16 elongate eggs. Females sometimes nest together, laying as many as 85 eggs in rotting vegetation.

SOUTHERN GREEN SNAKE *Philothamnus occidentalis* 70–110cm

Due to its *bright green body,* this snake is often mistaken for a Boomslang. However, it lacks fangs or venom and has *smooth body scales.* The ventral and subcaudal scales may also be *weakly keeled.* It has *large eyes* and *2 pairs of temporals on each side of the head.* This snake is an active and alert hunter of small frogs and lizards in low trees and bushes. It does not constrict prey, it simply swallows it alive. Lays up to 8 elongate eggs in summer.

GREEN WATER SNAKE *Philothamnus hoplogaster* 60–90cm

Very similar in habits, appearance and distribution to Southern Green Snake, and impossible to distinguish unless in the hand. This species has a *rounder head,* the *temporals are not paired,* and the *ventrals and subcaudal scales lack keels.* Some individuals, particularly juveniles, may have *black crossbars on the forebody.* This snake is an active swimmer that favours pans and backwaters, where it hunts small frogs. This gentle species rarely attempts to bite and does not inflate the throat in threat. Lays 3–8 elongate eggs in spring.

BOOMSLANG *Dispholidus typus* 120–200cm

Top: Adult male; above: Juvenile

One of the most characteristic snakes of southern Africa, although absent from the drier, relatively treeless western regions. Juveniles have chocolate-coloured heads, bright emerald eyes, white throats and cryptic, twig-coloured bodies. Females remain drab olive, while males may be very variable in colour. At about 1m in length they may become mottled in black and gold, or uniform rust-red or even powdery blue in the south. From Zululand north, especially beyond the Limpopo River, males are usually bright green. All can easily be distinguished by the *rounded head* with *very large eyes* and *oblique, strongly keeled body scales*. It is a dangerous but shy diurnal snake that hunts chameleons and small birds. When disturbed, it inflates the throat and will bite readily. The venom prevents blood clotting and death may follow in 1–3 days unless a specific antivenin or blood transfusions are given. Lays 10–15, sometimes up to 23, eggs in soft soil or in a tree hollow.

TWIG SNAKE 💀 *Thelotornis capensis*   80–120cm

Johan Marais

The *very thin, elongate body, lance-like head* and *twig-like body coloration* make this snake unmistakable. The *large eyes have keyhole-shaped pupils*. The body scales are *feebly keeled* and the *tail is very long*. The grey-brown body has fine black and pink flecks and a series of diagonal pale blotches. The *crown of the head is pale blue-green*, heavily speckled with black and sometimes pink, with a black and rust red stripe from the snout, through the eye, to the neck. This snake is completely arboreal and hunts lizards and small birds, which are swallowed while the snake hangs downwards among the branches. Lays 4–18 elongate eggs in summer. This species has potent venom that may cause death from internal bleeding.

RED-LIPPED SNAKE *Crotaphopeltis hotamboeia*   60–75cm

This species is easily distinguished from all other local snakes by its *bright red-orange lips*. However, in northern populations this colour fades and the *glossy black temporal region* and *white flecks on the olive body* are more diagnostic. The large eyes in the broad head have *vertical pupils*. This snake is a nocturnal inhabitant of marshy areas, where it hunts small frogs. Bad-tempered, it gives a dramatic threat by flattening the head to accentuate the red lips. However, it is harmless, although the long back fangs can inflict deep punctures. Lays 6–19 eggs in early spring.

COBRAS AND RELATIVES Family Elapidae

These snakes are relatively large with big, hollow, front fangs that are not hinged. The body is usually covered in smooth scales, and the head has large, symmetrical scales. Most species lay eggs and many have powerful venoms that can cause death from paralysis.

YELLOW-BELLIED SEA SNAKE ☠ *Hydrophis platurus* 60–80cm

Sea snakes are common in the East Indies, but this is the only species that enters southern African coastal waters. Vagrants are washed south in the Agulhas Current from tropical seas around Madagascar. A hapless voyager, it weakens in our cool waters, and eventually 'wrecks' when washed onto the eastern beaches by onshore winds. The *bright yellow and black stripes*, *flat head*, and *oar-like tail* are unmistakable. This snake drifts in surface currents, ambushing small fish sheltering in floating debris. Gives birth to 3–5 young in the surface waves. The powerful venom causes paralysis, but few deaths have been recorded.

GÜNTHER'S GARTER SNAKE ☠ *Elapsoidea guentheri* 40–50cm

Colin Tilbury

This rare snake is locally restricted to miombo woodland in central and northern Zimbabwe. The *snout is rounded*, and *4 lower labials touch the anterior chin shields*. Juveniles are black with *16–20 white crossbars* on the body and *2–4 bands* on the tail. In adults, these fade to leave narrow, paired bands that may be absent in large specimens. Like other garter snakes, their diet is varied and includes other snakes and even flying termites. Nothing is known of the venom. Lays up to 10 eggs in summer.

SUNDEVALL'S GARTER SNAKE *Elapsoidea sundevalli*   50–90cm

Garter snakes are notoriously difficult to identify. There is little difference in scale counts between species, and the brightly banded juvenile pattern may be present, absent or modified in adults. This species is among the most cryptic. The snout is *slightly pointed*. Juveniles have *alternating bands of cream-pink and chocolate-brown*, separated by narrow white rings. The latter persist in adults in the south, but elsewhere all bands fade in adults, which may be uniform olive, slate-grey or black with a pink-buff belly. This species is slow-moving and nocturnal. It eats rodents, lizards and even other snakes. Lays up to 10 small eggs. This snake's venom is relatively mild, but should not be ignored.

BOULENGER'S GARTER SNAKE  *Elapsoidea boulengeri*   50–77cm

A slightly smaller species, with *rounded snout* and *3 lower labials touching the anterior chin shields*. Juveniles have *white heads* and *12–17 narrow white bands on the black back*. In adults (over 20cm)

the pale bands darken in the centre to leave *very narrow paired bands*, which may disappear completely in large adults. This is a rare, shy snake that eats small vertebrates, including other snakes, and is prone to cannibalism in captivity. Although it will hiss when disturbed, it does not rear or spread a hood. Lays 4–8 eggs in early summer.

CORAL SHIELD COBRA ☠ *Aspidelaps lubricus*   40–75cm

An attractive, small, cobra-like snake that can be identified by the *large rostral scale* on the nose. Southern populations have a *brightly black-banded orange body*, but in northern Namibia adults become drabber and larger. There are *19 smooth midbody scale*

rows. This snake is a nocturnal hunter in semi-desert, and eats small lizards and rodents. Lays 3–11 eggs in summer. When disturbed, this snake rears the forebody, and spreads a *very narrow hood*. The venom is relatively mild, but has caused death. In captivity it feeds well, but remains bad-tempered.

SHIELD COBRA ☠ *Aspidelaps scutatus*   45–75cm

This short, thickset snake is less brightly coloured than the Coral Shield Cobra, and has a much larger, *bulldozer-like rostral scale*. The scales are in *21–25 rows at midbody*, and become *heavily keeled on the hindbody*. The *head and neck are usually black*, with a *white throat band*. Eastern populations have faint dorsal blotches on the

warm orange body. This snake burrows in loose sand, emerging at night to feed on rodents and frogs. When disturbed, it may rear and spread a *narrow hood*. It huffs and puffs a lot, but usually strikes with a closed mouth. Lays 4–10 eggs, around which the female may coil.

RINKHALS ☠ *Hemachatus haemachatus* 90–150cm

Johan Marais

Above: Unbanded phase
Left: Banded phase

This large, stout cobra is named after the characteristic 2 or 3 *white throat bands*. It differs from other cobras in having *keeled body scales* and giving birth to as many as 63 young in autumn. Juveniles are conspicuously banded, with about *40 irregular, alternating black and tan bands*. These may fade with age, and adults on the highveld are dirty grey-black with no trace of banding. Adults in Zimbabwe and the Eastern Cape may remain brightly banded, with yellowish-orange bands. This species is mainly nocturnal and hunts toads and small rodents in damp grassland. Its toxic venom is potentially fatal. It can spit venom up to 3m in defence. It may also sham death, rolling onto its back with the tongue hanging out of an open mouth.

BLACK SPITTING COBRA ☠ *Naja nigricincta woodi* 130–200cm

Bryan Marais

This large, *diurnal* race is found from southern Namibia south to Ceres. It is distinguished by its *black coloration* and in having *221–228 ventral scales*. Juveniles are grey with a black head and throat. It is an active hunter of rodents, lizards and even other snakes among the rock outcrops and dry water courses of the succulent Karoo. It spits venom willingly, but few bites are known. Breeding poorly known; lays up to 22 eggs, and hatchlings measure 35–40cm.

ZEBRA COBRA/WESTERN BARRED SPITTING COBRA ☠
Naja nigricincta nigricincta 120–180cm

The *narrowly banded pattern* is superfically similar to that of the Rinkhals (p.52), but it has *7–21 rows of smooth midbody scales*. The head is broad with a *rounded snout*. The pale grey to pink-brown body has *51–86 black bands on the back* and *13–32 bands on the tail*. There is a broad, *dark throat band*. This snake is nocturnal and hunts frogs and rodents in the more well-watered regions of northern Namibia. It is capable of spitting toxic venom up to 2.5m, and bites result in extensive skin necrosis that heals slowly and often requires skin grafts. Lays 10–20 eggs.

MOZAMBIQUE SPITTING COBRA ☠ *Naja mossambica*   90–150cm

This small, easily provoked spitting cobra has a *blunt head* and *23–25 midbody scale rows*. The *pink-grey to dark olive body* has each scale *edged with black*, while the *pinkish belly* may have *irregular black crossbars or blotches* on the throat. This snake's diet is varied, and mice, lizards, amphibians and even grasshoppers may be eaten. Lays 10–22 eggs in summer.

Due to its nocturnal habits, this species is responsible for many snake bites in Zululand and the lowveld, but fatalities are rare. When disturbed, it spreads a broad hood and spits readily.

FOREST COBRA ☠ *Naja melanoleuca*   180–270cm

André Coetzer

This is the largest and most impressive cobra in Africa. The slender body has *19 rows of glossy scales*. The head and forebody are *yellow-brown, heavily speckled in black*, while the *tail is shiny blue-black*. The lower labials are often *white with black edges*, particularly in northern populations. This snake inhabits rainforest, and is locally restricted to northern Zululand and the Zimbabwe eastern escarpment. Although mainly nocturnal, it may bask in the evening. It is fond of water and eats small vertebrates, including fish. When cornered, it will rear, spread a narrow hood, and bite readily. Bites are very rare, but serious emergencies. Lays up to 26 eggs, and hatchlings measure 30–40cm.

CAPE COBRA ☠ *Naja nivea*

120–180cm

A slender, nervous cobra that has a very toxic venom. It has a *broad head* and *smooth, but dull scales in 19–21 rows* at midbody. Juveniles are dirty yellow, speckled with dark brown, and have a *broad black throat band*. Adult coloration varies, from uniform yellow (Kalahari region) to dark mahogany (Namaqualand), although most specimens are heavily flecked in dark brown. The black throat band fades with age. It is an active, diurnal hunter along rocky ridges and river courses in the western arid region. Small vertebrates, including other snakes, form the main diet, and these snakes often raid Sociable Weaver nests in the Kalahari. Lays 8–20 large eggs underground. This cobra spreads a broad hood and bites willingly, although it does not spit venom.

SNOUTED COBRA ☠ *Naja annulifera*

150–250cm

A *stout, large-headed* cobra, characterized by having a row of scales *(suboculars)* between the eye and upper labials. The body is usually yellowish-brown, with old specimens becoming blue-black. There is a banded phase, with 7–9 broad yellow bands. A *dark throat band* is conspicuous

in juveniles. This snake is nocturnal, emerging at dusk to hunt small vertebrates. It regularly eats other snakes, particularly Puff Adders (p.58). Lays 8–33 large eggs in summer. It spreads a broad hood and bites readily, but does not spit. This snake may sham death when restrained. The venom causes death from respiratory failure.

BLACK MAMBA ☠ *Dendroaspis polylepis* 200–450cm

This is Africa's most feared snake. It is a *very large, slender* snake with a *coffin-shaped head* and *smooth, but dull scales.* The body is dirty grey, sometimes olive, with black blotches on the pale grey-green belly. The *mouth lining is black.* It is an active, mainly terrestrial species that occasionally climbs trees in search of food. Rats and dassies form the main diet; they are pursued and repeatedly stabbed until they succumb to the very toxic venom. When disturbed, this snake rears the forebody, gapes widely, spreads a very narrow hood, and gives a hollow hiss. Heed the warning! Lays a small clutch of 12–18 large eggs.

GREEN MAMBA ☠ *Dendroaspis angusticeps* 180–250cm

A smaller, more *slender* and *arboreal* relative of the Black Mamba. The body is *brilliant green*, and the *mouth lining is white*. Locally, it is restricted to the forests of coastal KwaZulu-Natal and the eastern escarpment of Zimbabwe. It lives in the upper forest canopy, ambushing small mammals and birds as it lies in wait in the canopy. This snake is shy and rarely seen. Bites are very rare, and although they are not as dangerous as those of the black mamba, they are still serious emergencies. Lays up to 10 eggs in a hollow log or leaf litter in summer. **V**

ADDERS AND VIPERS Family Viperidae

These snakes are characterized by their large, hollow, hinged front fangs through which venom is injected. The body is usually stout with a short tail, and the head is wide, with small, irregular scales on the crown. This is not the case in night adders, which also lay eggs, while most other adders are viviparous.

RHOMBIC NIGHT ADDER ☠ *Causus rhombeatus* 40–90cm

A stout snake, although thin for an adder, with a *rounded snout* and *soft, feebly keeled scales*. There are *large, paired scales on top of the head*. The grey-pink body and tail have *20–30 dark, pale-edged rhombic blotches*, and there is a characteristic *dark V-shape on the back of the head*. This snake inhabits moist situations in the eastern regions, emerging at night to feed on toads. Lays 15–26 eggs in summer. Although aggressive when first caught, this adder tames readily. The mild venom causes swelling but there have been few recorded deaths.

SNOUTED NIGHT ADDER ☠ *Causus defilippii* 30–43cm

Similar in build and coloration to the Rhombic Night Adder, although this species is *smaller* and has *triangular dorsal blotches*. This adder also has a pointed and upturned snout. It is

common in the lowveld, although tolerates more arid savanna in Zimbabwe. This snake feeds almost exclusively on small amphibians. Lays small clutches of 6–8 eggs in summer. This species' venom is mild, and causes little more than local swelling and pain.

PUFF ADDER ☠ *Bitis arietans*

70–90cm

A large, *thick-bodied*, sluggish snake that has a *short tail* and a *triangular head covered in small scales*. The body is yellow-brown to pale brown, with numerous *dark, pale-edged chevrons* on the back. Males are more brightly coloured than females. This snake hides at the base of a bush to ambush small mammals. It is found throughout the region, but is absent from desert and high mountains. Gives birth to about 20–30 young in late summer. This is a very dangerous snake that is responsible for many bites, although these are only rarely fatal. It gives a deep warning hiss.

GABOON ADDER ☠ *Bitis gabonica*

80–120cm

Another *large, heavy* adder with a *triangular head covered in small scales*. The body has an attractive *geometric pattern of purple, brown and pastel colours*, while the pale head has a *thin, dark central line* and *2 dark triangles radiating backwards from the eye to the lip*. It is perfectly camouflaged when sheltering among leaf litter on the forest floor. Although docile and rarely biting, this adder should always be treated with respect. Gives birth to up to 43 young in late summer. Locally, it is restricted to the coastal forests of northern KwaZulu-Natal and the escarpment forests of eastern Zimbabwe, where it is endangered due to habitat destruction. **NT**

BERG ADDER ☠ *Bitis atropos* complex 30–55cm

Typical coloration of populations from: eastern highlands of Zimbabwe (top), Cape Fold Mountains (above left) and eastern escarpment (above right)

This small adder is found in isolated populations in the escarpment mountains, from Inyanga in Zimbabwe to the Cederberg in the southwestern Cape. Most are *boldly patterned* in grey and blue-black, but the colour varies between populations, and eastern escarpment snakes are browner.
The head is *elongate, lacks horns*, and has a *dark arrowhead* on the crown. The stout body is covered in *keeled scales in 29–33 rows at midbody*. These snakes hunt small vertebrates, including frogs and lizards, with large females taking rodents. They are irascible, hissing and striking readily. Venom varies in toxicity and symptoms between populations. Some bites cause only drooping eyelids and the loss of taste and smell, but other bites may lead to swelling and necrosis. Mating occurs in autumn and up to 16 young are born in late summer.

PLAIN MOUNTAIN ADDER *Bitis inornata*   25–35cm

 A small, fat adder that *lacks horns* above the eyes, and has *27–31 midbody scale rows*. The back is *dull brown with fainter dark blotches*. The belly is dirty cream with blotches restricted to the sides. This snake is poorly known and apparently restricted to the montane grassland of the Compassberg and Sneeuberg north of Graaff-Reinet. It is active during the early morning and evening, and hides among small stones and grass tussocks to ambush passing lizards, particularly skinks and sand lizards. Gives birth to 6–8 young in late summer. **E**

RED ADDER *Bitis rubida*   25–42cm

 A small adder that may have *a small tuft of horns above the eyes*, although these may be absent. It has *25–29 midbody scale rows*. Coloration is varied: snakes from the Cederberg are very red with only a vague pattern, while those from the Little Karoo and Sutherland are dull brown to grey-brown with 18–20 dark blotches. This species occurs in scattered populations and is poorly known. It is active during the early morning and evening, and feeds on lizards, although large females may take mice. Gives birth to up to 10 young in late summer.

MANY-HORNED ADDER   *Bitis cornuta*   30–54cm

One of the larger small adders in the region, easily recognized by the *blotched grey-black dorsal pattern*, and a *tuft of 2–4 large, horn-like scales above each eye*. Symmetrical dark markings on the crown of the head may fuse to form an *arrowhead-shape*. This adder shelters under rocks and in rodent burrows, ambushing rodents and lizards. In summer it is most active during the early morning and evening. It is found mainly in the coastal regions of the western Cape and southern Namibia. Gives birth to about 4–10 young in late summer. No deaths are recorded but the venom is known to be very toxic.

ALBANY ADDER   *Bitis albanica*   25–30cm

A very small adder that has *a small tuft of horns above the eyes*, and has 27–29 midbody scale rows. The back is boldly marked in grey and black with *15–22 rectangular dark blotches*. There is a *prominent dark arrow mark* on the top of the head. This adder feeds on small lizards, particularly skinks and sand lizards. It is Critically Endangered and restricted to one small population in Algoa Bay. Nothing is known of its reproduction or venom. **CE**

HORNED ADDER ☠ *Bitis caudalis* 25–60cm

Colour variations from a variety of localities: Karasberg, southern Namibia (top); Tsumeb, northern Namibia (middle left); Ombasu Ost, northern Namibia (middle right); Blouberg, Limpopo province (bottom)

 This small adder is easily recognized by the *single horn above each eye*. The body is blotched and the ground colour may vary regionally, from pale grey in Etosha, buff to orange-brown in the Kalahari, to grey-olive to pale brown in the Karoo and Northern Cape. The head has a *dark V- or hourglass-shape* on the crown. The *creamy white belly is always unpatterned*. It is a common snake of the western arid regions, where it shuffles into sand at the base of a bush. There, it lies with only the top of the head and eyes visible, waiting for lizards to approach within striking distance. Large females may also eat small mice and gerbils. Usually 4–10 young are born in late summer, but a large female gave birth to 27 young. The venom is mild and no deaths have been reported.

PÉRINGUEY'S ADDER ☠ *Bitis peringueyi* 20–25cm

This species is endemic to the Namib Desert and specialized for life in the shifting, windblown sands. It is easily identified by its *small size* and the eyes positioned *on top of the flattened head*. The *subcaudal scales are smooth*, except for small keels towards the tip. The body is pale or reddish-brown with faint dark spots. It is famous for its ability to 'sidewind', moving in smooth lateral curves that lift most of the body off the hot sand. This snake shuffles into loose sand, leaving only the eyes exposed, ambushing small lizards from this position. It often has a black tail tip, which may be waved to lure lizards into striking range. Gives birth to 3–10 very small young (8–14cm) in late summer.

NAMAQUA DWARF ADDER ☠ *Bitis schneideri* 18–24cm

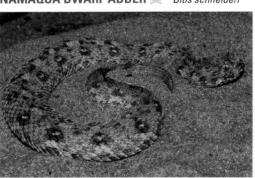

The smallest adder in the world, and similar in appearance and habits to Péringuey's Adder. However, this species' eyes are placed on the *side of the head* and the *subcaudal scales are more strongly keeled*. It inhabits more compacted coastal sands in Namaqualand and the southern dune sea of Namibia. Small lizards and sometimes frogs are eaten. Gives birth to 3 or 4 small young in late summer. This adder will hiss and strike in defence, but its venom is very mild and there have been no serious injuries.

DESERT MOUNTAIN ADDER ☠ *Bitis xeropaga* 40–60cm

Living in the inhospitable mountains bordering the lower Orange River, this small, *relatively slender* adder is poorly known. It has a ridge above each eye, but these bear *no horns*. The *subcaudal scales are smooth* and the *belly is pale grey patterned with dark speckles*. The *buff-grey back has 16–34 dark and pale bars*. It is a rock-living species that does not shuffle into sand or sidewind. It prefers succulent vegetated rocky slopes, where it catches small rodents and lizards. There have been no recorded bites, but the snake should be treated with care. Gives birth to 4 or 5 young in late summer.

SWAMP VIPER ☠ *Proatheris superciliaris* 40–60cm

Johannes Penner

A medium-sized adder, with a robust body and *elongate head*. Although most of the head shields are fragmented, there is a *large scale above each eye*. The grey-brown body has *3 rows of blackish spots*,

separated by *yellowish bars*. The tail is *yellow-orange* below. Females grow larger than males. This species is restricted to low-lying marshes in the floodplain of the Zambezi River, where it lives in rodent burrows, emerging at night to feed on small frogs. Gives birth to 3–8 young at the start of the rainy season in early summer.

LIZARDS

SKINKS Family Scincidae

A large, diverse family with numerous legless species. They have shiny, overlapping scales with an internal bony layer (osteoderms). This flexible armour allows them to burrow underground and live in rock cracks. The head has large, symmetrical scales and the tail can be shed and regenerated.

GIANT LEGLESS SKINK *Acontias plumbeus* 35–45cm

This legless skink is one of the largest in the world. Like many members of the genus, it *retains eyelids*. The broad head has an *elongate, steel-grey snout*. The *uniform black* coloration and *large size* are diagnostic. This species prefers leaf litter in moist situations, where it burrows looking for invertebrates, although it will also eat burrowing frogs and even nestling rodents. Gives birth to 2–14 young in late summer. It grows slowly, but is easily kept in captivity, feeding on mince or pet food. It is restricted to the eastern coastal regions, and inland escarpment forests and adjacent grassland.

SHORT-HEADED LEGLESS SKINK *Acontias breviceps* 20–23cm

A medium-sized legless skink that can be distinguished by its *broad head with rounded snout*, *opaque lower eyelid*, *enlarged scales beneath the tail*, and *spotted belly*. The body is olive to light brown, sometimes with a speckled appearance due to dark brown to black spots on each scale. This legless skink

burrows underground in firm soils searching for earthworms and insect larvae. Gives birth to 2 or 3 live young in late summer. Known from isolated populations in the eastern escarpment and the northern parts of the Eastern Cape.

CAPE LEGLESS SKINK *Acontias meleagris* 20–26cm

Widely distributed in the southern Cape, this medium-sized legless skink is often found in dry, sandy soils beneath stones or dead trees. It has a *slender head and body*, with a *rounded snout* and *blunt tail. The lower eyelid is opaque.* The body is golden brown, often with a dark spot on each scale in western specimens. In the east, these spots may fuse to form longitudinal stripes. This species is usually associated with richer soils along dry river courses and valley floors. Gives birth to up to 4 young in late summer.

STRIPED LEGLESS SKINK *Acontias kgalagadi* 12–18cm

A small legless skink with a characteristic *flattened, spade-like edge to the snout.* The *eye is vestigial,* just a small dark spot beneath the scales. The scales are in *14 rows at midbody.* Coloration is varied, but most specimens have a *light orange-yellow back with 4–8 thin longitudinal stripes.* Occasional individuals

from throughout the range are all black. This species may be locally common in dunes and sandy clumps at the base of bushes, where it burrows in loose sand for insects. Gives birth to 1 or 2 large young in summer.

NAMAQUA LEGLESS SKINK *Acontias namaquensis* 20–26cm

 Restricted to Namaqualand, this medium-sized legless skink is often found in dry sandy soils beneath stones or dead trees. It has a *rounded snout* and *longish tail*. The *lower eyelid is opaque* and has *3 suboculars*. The body is *pale olive-brown, each scale with a dark edge*. This species is usually associated with richer soils along dry river courses and valley floors. Gives birth to 2 or 3 young in late summer.

LITTORAL LEGLESS SKINK *Acontias litoralis* 12–15cm

 This small legless skink is restricted to sandy soils on the West Coast from Dabras south to Elandsbaai. It has a slender head and body, and the snout has a *horizontal spade-like edge*. The *lower eyelid is transparent*. The *tail is flattened below*.

 The *body is yellow*, usually with a *broad purple-brown band down the spine*. Some individuals are all yellow with a dark eye stripe. This legless skink burrows in sparsely vegetated coastal dunes searching for insects. Gives birth to 1 or 2 large young in summer.

GOLDEN BLIND LEGLESS SKINK *Acontias aurantiacus* 15–20cm

 These skinks are very varied and are probably a complex of cryptic species. The body is thick and the snout is rounded (southern populations) to slightly flattened (northern populations). The head shields are reduced in number, with *only 2 unpaired shields behind the rostral*. The eye is just a *black spot below the head scales*. There are *12 scale rows at midbody*. The body is usually *uniform pale orange or yellow*, paler below, and sometimes with scattered spots below the tail. Some populations develop dorsal stripes on the back. Inhabits coastal sands and sandveld in lower Limpopo valley, coastal Mozambique and northern Zululand. It gives birth to a few small young.

LOMI'S BLIND LEGLESS SKINK *Typhlosaurus lomiae* 11–14cm

 A small blind species with an *elongate and flattened snout*. The head shields are reduced, with only *2 unpaired shields* behind *the large rostral*. The eye is just a *black spot below the head scales*. There are *12 scale rows at midbody*. The body lacks pigmentation, being usually flesh-coloured, often with a yellow-orange tinge on the back. This skink burrows in sand at the base of bushes in sparsely vegetated coastal dunes in Namaqualand. **NT**

CUVIER'S BLIND LEGLESS SKINK *Typhlosaurus caecus* 18–22cm

A thin blind species with a *slightly flattened but rounded snout*. The *mental scale is heart-shaped*, with a *median cleft*, and there are *207–230 ventrals*. The eye is just a *black spot below the head scales*. The body is light yellow-orange with a light pink band behind the head and an orange-pink belly. This species burrows in sand in sparsely vegetated coastal dunes along the West Coast. Gives birth to 1, possibly 2, young in summer.

WORM-LIKE BLIND LEGLESS SKINK *Typhlosaurus vermis* 20–27cm

A *very thin* blind species with a *slightly flattened but rounded snout*. The head shields are reduced, with only *2 unpaired shields* behind the *large rostral*. The eye is just a *black spot below the head scales*. There are *12–14 scale rows at midbody*. The body lacks pigmentation and is flesh-coloured above and below. This species burrows in sparsely vegetated coastal dunes from the Orange River south to Spoeg River. Gives birth to 2 or 3 thin young in summer.

CAPE DWARF BURROWING SKINK *Scelotes caffer* 9–12cm

A *tiny, thin-bodied* skink found in scattered populations in the Eastern Cape, West Coast and Little Karoo. It has *well-developed fore- and hindlimbs*, each with *3 minute toes*. The *lower eyelid is transparent*. The *tail is longer than the body*. Each scale of the *olive-grey body* is dark-centred. The *flanks are dark* and the *tail bluish-grey*. It is found beneath stones and among dead aloe stems and other plant debris. It wiggles rapidly when exposed. Gives birth to 1 or 2 young in December and January.

HEWITT'S DWARF BURROWING SKINK
Scelotes bidigittatus 12–15cm

Another small species that *lacks forelimbs*, but that has *2 toes on each of the small hindlimbs*. The *snout is rounded* and the *tail is as long as or slightly longer than the body*. Each scale of the dark brown body has a dark spot, and there is a well-defined *pale dorsolateral stripe*. The *tail is metallic blue*. This species is found among dead leaves or under rotting logs in lowveld or coastal bush. Restricted to the lowveld and northern Zululand. Gives birth to 1 or 2 young in late summer.

SILVERY DWARF BURROWING SKINK *Scelotes bipes* 11–14cm

A small burrowing skink of the southwestern Cape coastal region. It *lacks forelimbs*, and the *minute hindlimbs each have 2 toes*. The head is flattened with *minute ear openings*. The *lower eyelid is transparent*. There are *18 scale rows at midbody* and the *tail is slightly shorter than the body*. The silver-grey body is tinged with buff, and each scale is dark-centred. The greyish-white belly is lightly speckled. It is usually found beneath litter just above the high-water mark. Gives birth to 1 or 2 young in March or April.

WESTERN DWARF BURROWING SKINK
Scelotes capensis   9–11cm

Within its range this small burrowing skink can be confused with nothing else. Its *very bright blue tail* and the functional, but *minute 5-toed limbs* are diagnostic. There are *22 midbody scale rows* and the undamaged *tail is as long as the body*. Regenerated tails are usually much shorter than the body. The body is olive-brown with a coppery sheen, often with a lighter dorsolateral stripe on each side. This species can be found in moist soils beneath rocks, and particularly among decaying aloes. It is restricted to the moister mountain slopes of southern Namibia, just entering the Richtersveld. Its biology is poorly known.

WHITE-BELLIED DWARF BURROWING SKINK
Scelotes limpopoensis albiventris   10–13cm

A small burrowing skink with a very small range in the Soutpansberg region. There are only *2 toes on the forelimbs,* and *4 on the hindlimbs.* The *lower eyelid is semi-transparent.* There are *20–22 scale rows at midbody* and the *tail is slightly longer than the body.* The body is striped, with a *broad, dark brown band along the backbone.* The *belly is uniform white.* This burrowing skink forages among rocks and dead logs on sandy soil. Gives birth to 2 young in November. **NT**

KALAHARI BURROWING SKINK   *Typhlacontias rohani*   12–14cm

A slender burrowing skink that *lacks limbs or ear openings.* The eyes have *no eyelids,* but are not covered by the head shields. There are *18 scale rows at midbody* and the *tail is short.* The body is buff-coloured and striped, with a *vague brown band along the backbone.* The *belly is white at the edges, darker in the centre.* This skink is common under logs and vegetation on sandy soils in the northern Kalahari. Gives birth to 3 or 4 young in late summer.

COASTAL RAG SKINK *Cryptoblepharus africanus*   8–10cm

This small, slender skink is restricted to a few coastal rock outcrops on the eastern seaboard from Black Rock, KwaZulu-Natal, to Kenya. The *large eyes have immovable eyelids*, each with *a transparent spectacle*. The body is covered with smooth, close-fitting scales in *26–29 rows at midbody*, and the tail tapers to a fine point. The *blackish-bronze back has numerous pale spots* on the flanks and legs. It is a diurnal species that forages on intertidal rocks to catch small crustaceans, and even small fish. It swims readily, and dives into shallow pools to escape predators. Lays 1 or 2 eggs in sand. **E**

SUNDEVALL'S WRITHING SKINK *Mochlus sundevallii*   15–18cm

A small, *fat-bodied* skink that wriggles among leaf litter and loose sand. It has *moveable eyelids* and a *fat tail*. The bronze body appears speckled due to a small spot on each scale. This species is common in the northern savannas, where it feeds on termites and insects around rotting logs. Lays 2–6 soft-shelled eggs under a stone or in an old termite nest. The tail of this species was once prized as a cure for snakebite.

WESTERN ROCK SKINK *Trachylepis sulcata* 16–20cm

One of the commonest rock-living lizards in the Karoo and western arid region. It is a slender, flattened skink, with a *window in the lower eyelid*. Females and juveniles are olive-brown with *6 dirty gold stripes*. Breeding males vary in colour regionally. In the Karoo they turn jet black, with a heavily speckled throat; in Namaqualand and Namibia the males are also black, but with varying amounts of dirty bronze on the hindbody and tail. They shelter, sometimes communally, under large rock flakes. Gives birth to 3–5 young in late summer.

WEDGE-SNOUTED SKINK *Trachylepis acutilabris* 13–15cm

Easily confused with sand lizards, this small skink has close-fitting, shiny scales and a *flattened snout* with a *sharp edge to the upper lip*. The *ear openings are covered with long, sharp*

lobes. The light brown body has dark spots and white flecks that form short bands, and usually a pale dorsal stripe. This skink is a sit-and-wait predator, dashing from the shade of a small bush to seize insects. At night it shelters in a small tunnel dug in sand at the base of a bush. This species is restricted to the western arid regions of Namibia, and north into Angola. It lays a small clutch of 3–6 eggs.

CAPE SKINK *Trachylepis capensis* 20–25cm

This is a familar garden lizard throughout South Africa. It is a *fat, almost obese*, skink, with a *window in the lower eyelid* and *32–36 midbody scale rows*. The light brown body has 3 pale stripes, between which are numerous dark bars. Some specimens are olive-grey and almost patternless. It digs tunnels in loose sand around rotting logs, feeding on insects on warm days. Most specimens give birth to 5–18 young in late summer, although some females lay eggs.

KALAHARI TREE SKINK *Trachylepis spilogaster* 18–22cm

A medium-sized skink with *30–36 midbody scale rows*. There is a *window in the lower eyelid*, and the *subocular just reaches the lip*. The *dark brown* body has a *pair of pale dorsolateral stripes* and *numerous scattered pale spots*. This species is arboreal and common in the western arid region. It prefers large acacia trees in dry riverbeds, particularly those with Sociable Weaver nests. It gives birth to 3–5 young.

RAINBOW SKINK *Trachylepis margaritifer* 18–24cm

A common large, brightly coloured skink with *42–44 midbody scale rows*. It forms large colonies on granite outcrops in the lowveld and Zimbabwe. The females and juveniles have *dark bodies with 3 bluish-white stripes and electric blue tails*. Breeding males become *green-brown*, with a *pearly white spot on each scale* and a *bright orange-brown tail*. Males fight over territories, but ignore juveniles and females. Lays 6–10 eggs in early summer.

RED-SIDED SKINK *Trachylepis homalocephala* 15–18cm

A small, elegant lizard, with a *boldly striped, shiny body*. In the breeding season males develop *bright red flanks*. There is a *small window in each lower eyelid* and *28–30 midbody scale rows*. This skink forages in leaf litter around the base vegetation, in coastal regions of

southern and Eastern Cape. There are relict populations on the inland mountains of the Cape and Mpumalanga where rainfall is higher. These skinks are common in gardens, but remain shy. Lays about 6 eggs in early summer.

VARIABLE SKINK *Trachylepis varia* 12–16cm

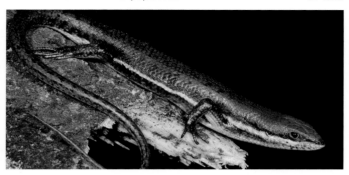

A smallish skink with a *rounded snout* and *30–36 midbody scale rows*. Characteristically, there is a *bright white lateral stripe* and *3 keels on the scales beneath the toes*. The dark, reddish-brown back may have black spots, and additional pale stripes. This skink hunts in broken ground, climbing on boulders and fallen trees. Insects, which form the main diet, are captured after a short dash from cover. This species is restricted mostly to the eastern regions. While mainly live-bearing, some females from the north may lay a single clutch of 6–12 eggs.

VARIEGATED SKINK *Trachylepis variegata* 11–14cm

Found throughout the western regions, this small, slender skink has *30–36 midbody scale rows* with only *3 keels on the scales*. The brown body *lacks an obvious white lateral stripe*. It has only a *single keel on the scales beneath the toes*. This skink is active around the base of rock outcrops, hunting small insects and spiders. Breeding males develop a rusty blush beneath the hindlimbs and tail. Gives birth to 2–4 young in late summer.

STRIPED SKINK *Trachylepis striata* complex   18–22cm

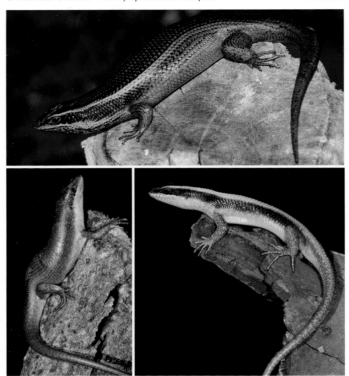

Sibling species in the Striped Skink complex: Speckled Rock Skink
(T. punctatissimus) (top); Wahlberg's Skink *(T. wahlbergii)* (above left);
Striped Skink *(T. striata)* (above right)

Widespread throughout the northern regions, these rather
dull skinks tame readily and are common on garden walls and
rockeries. *Midbody scale rows vary from 32–43* and colour
differs from region to region. The dark brown to black body may
have *bold white dorsolateral stripes* (in the east) or numerous
small, pale spots (in the south and central regions). The northern species has a
pale grey back that may have faint stripes, a black band extending from the eye
above the shoulder, and the breeding males develop yellow-orange throats.
Gives birth to 3–9 young at a time, females in the south breeding only in
summer, those further north breeding throughout the year.

WAHLBERG'S SNAKE-EYED SKINK
Panaspis wahlbergii   8–10cm

 A small skink, easily identified by its *immovable eyelid* and *grey-bronze body*, which may have *6 fine dark lines*. The smooth body scales are in *24–26 rows at midbody*. The belly is greyish-blue, except in breeding males when it turns pinkish-orange. This skink scuttles among grass roots and rotting logs, feeding on termites and small insects. It is short-lived, surviving only 10–14 months. Females lay 2–6 eggs in early summer.

SPECKLE-LIPPED SNAKE-EYED SKINK
Panaspis maculicollis   8–10cm

 Very similar to Wahlberg's Snake-eyed Skink, and easily identified by its *immovable eyelid* and grey-bronze body. The main distinguishing feature is the *series of black and white spots along the side of the neck*. This species is found in more arid savanna of the northern region. It lives in small colonies in leaf litter, feeding on termites and small insects. Females lay up to 3 eggs in midsummer, with hatchlings appearing in January.

OLD WORLD LIZARDS Family Lacertidae

These lizards are usually small with slender bodies and long tails. The body is covered with small, granular scales on the back, but larger, rectangular scales on the belly. The head has large, symmetrical scales and the tail can be shed and regenerated. At least 30 species occur in the region.

ANCHIETA'S DESERT LIZARD *Meroles anchietae* 10–12cm

The unusual *flattened snout with a sharp cutting edge* is unmistakable. The *flattened body* has a *silvery sheen* and the tail may have a few *black crossbars*. The body scales are small and granular, and the toes of the *long hindlimbs have*

a conspicuous fringe. These allow it to race at high speed over the hot sand. When disturbed, or to sleep, this lizard dives into loose sand on a dune slip face. Small insects and plant seeds form the main diet. It is restricted to the windblown sands of the Namib Desert. Lays a single egg 3 or 4 times a year.

WEDGE-SNOUTED DESERT LIZARD *Meroles cuneirostris* 13–15cm

Very similar in appearance and habits to Anchieta's Desert Lizard, but this species has more *red-orange coloration* and *prominent pale spots*. The *tail is not barred*.

The cutting edge of the flattened snout is less pronounced. This lizard is also restricted to the southern Namib Desert, and the 2 species only meet in the Lüderitz region. It is not specialized for life on large dunes, preferring low, vegetated dune hummocks. Males have a more blotched pattern. There is no distinct breeding season, and 2–4 eggs are laid in soft sand.

SMITH'S DESERT LIZARD *Meroles ctenodactylus* 15–18cm

Another sand-living species, similar in appearance and habits to Wedge-Snouted Desert Lizard, but *larger* and with a *sand-to red-coloured body*, sometimes with vague pale spots and dark flecks. A *pale lateral stripe* extends from the eye to the tail base. The *tail is not barred.* This species occurs from Little Namaqualand to Sossusvlei in the southern Namib Desert. It prefers valley floors with low, vegetated dune hummocks, waiting in a shaded spot to ambush insects. Lays 4–6 eggs in soft sand at the base of a bush.

SPOTTED DESERT LIZARD *Meroles suborbitalis* 12–14cm

A small sand lizard that *lacks a sharp digging edge to the snout.* The *supranasals are separated*, and the *toes have a feeble fringe.* It prefers flat, sparsely vegetated gravel plains. The back coloration is variable and often matches the local ground colour. It is usually mottled pink-grey to slate. Some populations may retain faded stripes from the juvenile colour pattern, while others may have pale lateral spots or yellow hindlimbs and tail base. Breeding is continuous and females lay 3–7 eggs throughout the year.

KNOX'S DESERT LIZARD *Meroles knoxii* 15–20cm

A small, active lizard that has a *rounded body*, but that *lacks a sharp edge on the snout* and has only a *weak fringe along the toes*. The *supranasals are in contact*. This species inhabits well-vegetated sand flats, sheltering in the shade of a grass tussock and making a quick dash to catch small insects. Juveniles are brightly striped in black and yellow. Adult males have a yellow flush to the lips, throat and anal region. This species is found in the coastal regions of the western Cape and Namaqualand. Lays 2 or 3 eggs in Western Cape; up to 6 eggs in Namaqualand.

ROUGH-SCALED DESERT LIZARD *Meroles squamulosus* 17–20cm

The most conspicuous feature of this small, active lizard is the *small, strongly keeled body scales*. The *snout lacks a sharp edge* and there is *no fringe along the toes*. The cryptically coloured *buff-brown body* has *narrow, dark crossbars or blotches* and *long rows of pale spots*. This species is widespread in the northern regions, where it shelters in a burrow in soft sand at the base of bushes. It is very short-lived, growing to maturity in 8–9 months and dying within 12–14 months after breeding. Lays 8–12 eggs in April–June.

BUSHVELD LIZARD *Heliobolus lugubris* 16–20cm

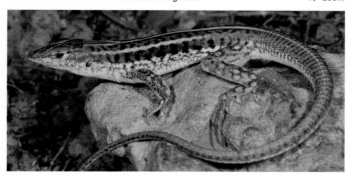

 A small lizard with a *well-developed collar*, and *small, keeled scales on the back*. The *long toes lack a fringe*. Adults have grey-tan to red-brown backs with vague crossbars and *3 pale dorsal stripes*. Hatchlings are very different, having a *jet black body with broken yellow-white stripes*, and a sand-coloured tail. They walk slowly with a stiff-legged gait and mimic distasteful oogpister beetles, which squirt a pungent acid when threatened. Lays 4–6 eggs in loose sand.

VHEMBE ROCK LIZARD *Vhembelacerta rupicola* 10–12cm

 A small lizard with *a well-developed collar*. The *subocular borders the lip*. The *body scales are smooth and granular*, and in about *36 rows at midbody*. The dark brown back has a *pair of reddish-brown stripes along the backbone*, and a *white dorsolateral stripe*. This lizard lives among rocks on the vegetated summit of the Soutpansberg. Lays a small clutch of 3 or 4 eggs beneath a sun-warmed rock slab in summer. **NT**

DELALANDE'S SANDVELD LIZARD *Nucras lalandii* 20–28cm

 A stout-bodied lizard with a *blunt snout* and a *thick tail*, which is *almost twice the body length*. The tail is used as a fat store, but is easily shed. There are *no enlarged scales under the forelimb*. The olive-grey body has *8–10 irregular rows of white, black-edged spots*. In adults the black edges may fuse to form broken crossbars. The belly is white with numerous black spots. This lizard spends long periods underground in long burrows dug beneath rock slabs or fallen logs in grassland. When food is plentiful, it emerges to eat insects and flying termites. Lays 4–9 eggs in summer.

STRIPED SANDVELD LIZARD *Nucras taeniolata* 18–20cm

A small species with *fine, granular body scales*. The *tail is about twice the body length*, and there are *6 or 7 enlarged scales under the forelimb*. The dark brown body has 8–11 fine cream stripes that are fainter along the backbone. The tail is orange-brown in adults, but brighter in juveniles. This lizard is usually found among fallen trees or plant debris in mesic thicket. It is rarely seen, and hunts for other lizards among thick vegetation at the base of bushes. Lays 4 or 5 eggs in summer. **NT**

WESTERN SANDVELD LIZARD *Nucras tessellata*   20–25cm

One of the region's most beautiful lizards. The *bright black-and-white barred flanks* and *long red tail* are unmistakable. These lizards are slow, terrestrial hunters in the western arid regions, emerging from burrows under stones. They are specialist feeders

 on scorpions and large beetles, which are dug from their retreats. While digging or searching for food, they are unable to spot predators. The bright red tail helps to direct attack away from the vulnerable head and body. Lays 3 or 4 eggs.

ORNATE SANDVELD LIZARD *Nucras ornata*   22–26cm

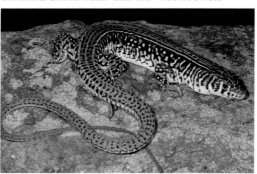

A large, graceful lizard with a *long, orange-brown tail* that is *more than twice the body length*. The light brown back has numerous rows of *white, black-edged spots*. The belly is white, with dark specks restricted to the sides. The

 juvenile is more brightly coloured, with a coral red tail. It is a fast-moving, terrestrial species that hunts among leaf litter at the edge of bushes. This species is found in the eastern regions from the Lebombo Mountains, through the lowveld to central Mozambique. Lays 5–7 eggs in midsummer.

BURCHELL'S SAND LIZARD *Pedioplanis burchelli* 14–16cm

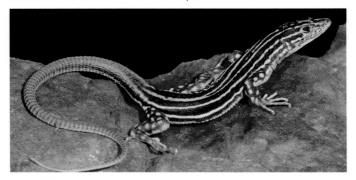

 This is one of the commonest terrestrial lizards in the grasslands and summit bedrock of the Cape and Lesotho mountains. Its *tail is only slightly longer than its body*, and a *distinct collar* and *faint gular fold* are present. Hatchlings are *vividly striped in black and gold*, with a *blue flush to the tail*. Colours fade to cryptic browns in adults, although faint stripes may still be visible. These lizards prefer exposed bedrock with scattered grass clumps, and shelter under rock slabs at night and during winter. Lays a small clutch of 4–6 eggs in soil under a rock slab in midsummer.

NAMAQUA SAND LIZARD *Pedioplanis namaquensis* 14–17cm

 A small, slender lizard with a *tail that is significantly longer than the body*. A *distinct collar* and *faint gular fold* are present, and an *enlarged crescent-shaped scale occurs above the ear*. As with Burchell's Sand Lizard, the juvenile is vividly striped but has a *pink-brown tail*. The adult becomes cryptically coloured in tans and browns, although in some regions they retain faint stripes. The tail remains orange-brown. This lizard is amazingly fast, shuttling between bushes on flat, sandy soil, catching insects. It shelters in a burrow dug in loose sand at the base of a bush. Lays 3–5 eggs in November.

PLAIN SAND LIZARD *Pedioplanis inornata*   14–16cm

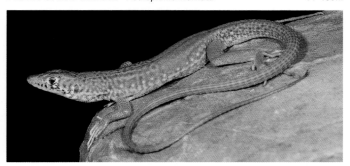

This rather drab, grey-brown lizard lives on the lower slopes of rocky oucrops in the western arid regions. The *tail is only slightly longer than the body*, and a *distinct collar* and *faint gular fold* are present. There is usually a *series of pale green spots on the flanks* and an *enlarged crescent-shaped scale occurs above the ear*. These lizards are active even on hot days, running on exposed bedrock in pursuit of small flying insects. They form small colonies in suitable habitat. Lays a small clutch of soft-shelled eggs in moist soil beneath a rock slab.

SPOTTED SAND LIZARD *Pedioplanis lineocellata*   13–17cm

Very similar to, and easily confused with, Plain Sand Lizard. This species differs in having a *series of pale blue spots on the flanks* and *lacks the enlarged crescent-shaped scale above the ear*. More widely distributed, it prefers rocky flats and broken ground. The back may retain juvenile stripes, particularly in Namaqualand specimens. These lizards are sit-and-wait hunters, grabbing small insects after a short dash from shaded cover. They shelter at night and in winter in a small chamber dug in soil beneath a flat stone. Lays 4–8 eggs in midsummer.

COMMON MOUNTAIN LIZARD *Tropidosaura montana* 12–15cm

 This secretive lizard may be locally common, but does not move far from thick cover and is therefore rarely seen. It has a *short head*, *relatively long tail*, and *spiny, overlapping body scales*. A *collar is absent*, but a *faint gular fold and a single preanal scale are present*. The olive body has a dark streak along the backbone, a pale dorsolateral stripe, and a series of pale yellow spots on the flanks. These become bright orange in the breeding season. The tail has a blue-green flush. This lizard lives and climbs among heathers and grass, where it is perfectly camouflaged. It is active in the early morning and evening, feeding on small insects. Lays a small clutch of 4 or 5 eggs in summer.

COTTRELL'S MOUNTAIN LIZARD *Tropidosaura cottrelli* 14–18cm

 Similar to the Common Mountain Lizard, but grows larger and has a *pair of preanal scales*. In the breeding season males become vividly coloured, with dark backs with scattered bright orange or green-blue spots, which may form bands. A light yellow stripe runs along the lower flank. The belly is bluish with large black blotches. This lizard is terrestrial and hunts insects in the montane grassland of the Drakensberg escarpment. It shelters in a tunnel that it digs in deep soil, and hibernates in this retreat during winter. It lays a small clutch of 3–5 eggs. **NT**

PLATED LIZARDS Family Gerrhosauridae

Endemic to Africa and Madagascar, more than half the known species of this small family found in southern Africa. They are diurnal, oviparous lizards, most having stout bodies, long tails and well-developed limbs. The body scales are rectangular and have osteoderms. A prominent lateral fold is characteristic.

DWARF PLATED LIZARD *Cordylosaurus subtessellatus*   12–14cm

This small, elegant lizard is easily recognized by the *long, bright blue tail and striped body*. It forages among succulent-covered rock outcrops, feeding on small insects. It frequently rests on its belly, raising its small feet off the ground. When threatened, this lizard wiggles among stones, and is very difficult to catch without dislodging the long tail. The tail continues to writhe after it is detached, thus distracting the would-be predator's attention. Lays 2 or 3 eggs in summer.

SHORT-LEGGED SEPS *Tetradactylus seps*   13–18cm

A small, *long-tailed lizard* with *reduced, but fully formed limbs*. The head, body and tail are dark bronze, speckled in black, and relieved only by *cream spots on the upper lips*, and *irregular bars on the neck*. This lizard is rarely seen, but locally common, favouring thick vegetation in moist clearings, either in coastal forest or on mountain slopes. Bees and grasshoppers form the main diet, and are captured during a short dash from cover. Lays 2 or 3 oval eggs.

COMMON LONG-TAILED SEPS *Tetradactylus tetradactylus* 18–24cm

As indicated by its species name, this thin, *snake-like lizard* has *only 4 toes on all of the very small limbs*. The *very long tail is 3 times as long as the body*. The back is olive with a *pair of dark brown dorsolateral stripes*. There are short black and white bars on the side of the neck. This lizard hunts in montane grassland or fynbos, catching small insects, particularly grasshoppers. At night it shelters in thick vegetation. Lays a small clutch of 3–5 eggs in summer.

FITZSIMONS' LONG-TAILED SEPS *Tetradactylus fitzsimonsi* 18–24cm

A thin, *snake-like lizard* that has *no forelimbs* and reduced *hindlimbs that are simple spikes*. The *very long tail is 3 times as long as the body*. The *back is olive* with a *dark brown stripe running down each scale row*. There are short black and white bars on the side of the neck. This lizard hunts small insects, particularly grasshoppers. It is restricted to coastal fynbos flats from Humansdorp to Port Elizabeth. Lays a small clutch of 3–5 eggs in summer. **V**

YELLOW-THROATED PLATED LIZARD
Gerrhosaurus flavigularis

25–35cm

With its small head, *long tail* and *bright yellow, dark-edged, lateral stripe on each flank*, this elegant, medium-sized lizard is unmistakable. Breeding males develop bright throats that may be yellow, red or even blue. It is common in the eastern regions, often adapting to suburban gardens. Terrestrial, living in a small burrow at the base of a bush, it is alert and difficult to catch without causing it to shed its tail. Lays 4–6 eggs in summer.

EASTERN BLACK-LINED PLATED LIZARD
Gerrhosaurus intermedius

30–35cm

A large, handsome plated lizard, similar to Yellow-throated Plated Lizard, but *more robust* and *lacking the lateral yellow line*. The brown body has a speckled appearance, and adults develop a bright blue flush to the throat and

flanks. This lizard lives in a burrow dug at the base of a shrub in the bushveld and northern Kalahari sandveld. With its powerful jaws it tackles large grasshoppers, beetles, and even scorpions. Lays 4–9 eggs that hatch in 10–15 weeks.

DESERT PLATED LIZARD *Gerrhosaurus skoogi* 20–25cm

Randy Babb

A large, unusual lizard that is endemic to the dune seas of the northern Namib Desert. It has a *spade-like snout* that it uses to dive into loose sand. The *short tail is only slightly longer than the body* and tapers abruptly to a fine point. Adults are ivory-coloured with scattered maroon blotches. The chin, throat and lower chest are black. Males grow larger than females. Juveniles are sand-coloured. This lizard is found in small colonies, and feeds on windblown insects and dry plant debris. It may spend up to 24 hours under the sand, sheltering from danger and temperature extremes. Lays 2–4 large eggs.

ROUGH-SCALED PLATED LIZARD *Broadleysaurus major* 30–40cm

A solid lizard, with a *short head* and *large eyes*. The *body scales are large and very rough*. The rounded, light brown body may have a light speckle and faint dorsolateral stripe. The chin and throat are pale cream. This lizard favours large, soil-filled cracks in well-wooded rock outcrops, and feeds on large insects. It also eats soft fruit and flowers, and will also eat any small lizards that it can catch. Lays a few (2–4) large, soft-shelled eggs in summer. It tames easily and settles well into captivity.

WESTERN GIANT PLATED LIZARD
Matobosaurus maltzhani 40–55cm

 A very large plated lizard. The *head and body are flattened,* the *subocular borders the lip,* and the *eye is red.* The *dorsal scales are small and only faintly keeled.* Adults have light brown backs, with irregular darker brown scale rows. The darker head has light yellow speckling. Breeding males develop a bluish flush to the chin and throat. Shy and difficult to approach, this species inhabits the upper slopes of large granite koppies in northern Namibia and Angola. Lays 2–5 large eggs in a soil-filled rock crack.

EASTERN GIANT PLATED LIZARD *Matobosaurus validus* 40–60cm

The largest plated lizard, exceeded in size only by monitor lizards. *The head and body are flattened,* the *subocular does not reach the lip,* and the *eye is red. The dorsal scales are small and only faintly keeled.* Juveniles are black with a series of yellow spots on the back, and bars on the flanks. These fade in adults, which have black backs with a light yellow speckle. Breeding males have a pink-purple flush to the chin and throat. Shy and difficult to approach, these lizards live on the upper slopes of large granite koppies in the northeastern region. They eat large insects, as well as flowers, soft fruit and leaves. Lays 2–5 large eggs in a soil-filled rock crack.

Stu Nielsen

GIRDLED LIZARDS Family Cordylidae

One of the few lizard families endemic to Africa. Girdled lizards have their main centre of radiation in southern Africa, where at least 40 species are present, including 3 unusual, snake-like species. The rectangular body scales are keeled and arranged in regular rows (girdles), and the body is usually flattened, almost box-like in cross-section. The head is flattened and has symmetrical head shields with embedded osteoderms. The tail in many species has whorls of spines and is easily shed, but can be regenerated. All except flat lizards give birth to a few live young.

CAPE GRASS LIZARD *Chamaesaura anguina*   35–40cm

An elongate, *snake-like lizard with minute, spike-like fore- and hindlimbs,* each with only 1–2 claws. The *body scales are rough and strongly keeled.* The *tail is 3 or 4 times as long as the body* and easily lost, but is rapidly regenerated. This lizard hunts grasshoppers and other insects in grassland, where its tan-and-brown body imparts perfect camouflage. Gives birth to a few small young in late summer.

HIGHVELD GRASS LIZARD *Chamaesaura aenea*   30–35cm

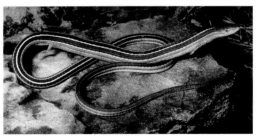

Very similar to Cape Grass Lizard, but with reduced, yet *perfectly formed feet, each with 5 clawed toes.* The *body scales are also slightly smaller,* although still strongly keeled. It is *more*

strongly striped, and the flanks may have a series of spots or a reddish-brown lateral stripe (from which the specific name, which means 'coppery', is derived). This species is restricted to the eastern escarpment grasslands, with an isolated population in the Winterberg. It gives birth to up to 12 young in summer. **NT**

CAPE GIRDLED LIZARD *Cordylus cordylus* 13–19cm

A very common species along the coastal rocks and mountain summits of the Cape. The body is usually mottled brown, often with a pale dorsal stripe. The *body scales are strongly keeled* and in *16–22 girdles*, while the *tail is spiny*. These lizards live in dense colonies where there are suitable rock cracks in which to shelter. The adults are aggressive and fight to form social hierarchies. If threatened, they jam into rock cracks by inflating the body and using the spiny tail to protect the head. Gives birth to 1–3 young in autumn.

HIGHVELD GIRDLED LIZARD *Cordylus vittifer* 14–17cm

Almost identical in appearance and habits to Cape Girdled Lizard, this species differs in having a *row of elongate scales on the nape of the neck*, and an *orange-red coloration*. A pale dorsal

stripe may also be present. This lizard is found among rocks on the highveld and adjacent grasslands. It basks on rocks in the morning sun, and catches beetles and grasshoppers with a short dash from the shelter of the rock crack. Gives birth to 1–3 young in autumn.

SOUTHERN TREE GIRDLED LIZARD *Cordylus jonesi* 12–16cm

 One of the arboreal girdled lizards, this small, round-bodied species shelters in hollow logs and under bark. The *scales are very rough*, but are *all smooth on the belly*. The back is lichen-coloured, with lighter flanks and belly. A dark lateral stripe extends from the neck along the side of the body, and the upper lip has a cream speckle. This lizard feeds on moths, spiders and winged termites. It lays down large fat reserves to tide it over winter. Gives birth to 2–4 young in summer.

LARGE-SCALED GIRDLED LIZARD *Cordylus macropholis* 14–17cm

 A small, round-bodied girdled lizard that inhabits coastal dunes and the strand line of the West Coast. The head has *6 strongly keeled occipitals*, and the *dorsal and ventral scales are also very rough,* and in only *16–18 girdles on the back*. The body is grey to olive-green with irregular dark markings. This lizard is terrestrial, sheltering at the base of succulent bushes, and catching beetles and grasshoppers with a short dash from shelter. Gives birth to 1 or 2 young April–May. **NT**

BLACK GIRDLED LIZARD *Cordylus niger* 13–19cm

A very common species among the coastal rocks of the Cape Peninsula and Saldanha Bay. The body is flattened and uniformly jet black, but paler below. This lizard is solitary, sheltering in small cracks. The black coloration enables it to absorb heat on overcast, foggy days. If threatened, this lizard retreats into rock cracks, using the spiny tail to protect the head. Gives birth to 1–3 young in autumn. **NT**

DWARF KAROO GIRDLED LIZARD *Cordylus aridus* 14–17cm

A *very small* and *very flat* girdled lizard that lives in the southern Karoo near Prince Albert. There are *no enlarged chin shields*, and the *obliquely keeled dorsal scales* are in *26–28 girdles*. The body, limbs and tail are dirty brown with irregular diffuse black markings. This lizard is shy and lives in vertical rock cracks in low, north-facing Dwyka tillite outcrops. Gives birth to 2 or 3 young in late summer.

PEERS' GIRDLED LIZARD *Namazonurus peersi* 15–17cm

A slender, *all black* girdled lizard that clambers effortlessly over the smooth granite outcrops of Little Namaqualand. The *body scales are strongly keeled* and the *nostrils are swollen*. This lizard is very visible when basking on the top of a large boulder, but is shy and retreats quickly to cover. Small groups of 3–7 specimens may share a large, sun-warmed crack, particularly in winter. Insects and caterpillars form the main diet. Gives birth to 2 or 3 young in autumn.

CAMPBELL'S GIRDLED LIZARD *Namazonurus campbelli* 15–17cm

This small, flattened girdled lizard is restricted to rocky hillsides of a small area in Great Namaqualand. The dorsal scales are keeled, particularly on the lower flanks, and in *27–31 girdles*. The back and tail are chestnut to light brown with irregular black and gold blotches, particularly along the backbone. The *head is darker, heavily speckled with golden spots*. Little is known of its biology, but it probably has 2 or 3 young in autumn.

KAROO GIRDLED LIZARD *Karusasaurus polyzonus* 20–25cm

Common throughout the western arid region, this *large, graceful girdled lizard* prefers broken ground. It is found in diffuse colonies, each lizard inhabiting a rock crack in a shattered boulder. It basks on a high point, making short forays to grab beetles or

grasshoppers. This species can be distinguished by the *smaller, more numerous girdles (38–46)*, and by a *black blotch on the sides of the neck*. Dorsal coloration is variable. Juveniles are tan-coloured, chequered with dark brown. This may be retained in adults, although all black, orange, and light blue populations are known. Gives birth to 2–4 young in late summer.

ARMADILLO GIRDLED LIZARD *Ouroborus cataphractus* 12–16cm

This thickset, *flattened* girdled lizard is famous for its defensive habit of rolling into a tight ball. It has a *broad head, very large, strongly keeled and often irregular girdles (15–17)*, and *large spines on the tail*. The *throat and belly are usually heavily blotched*. This species inhabits large cracks in low rock outcrops amid the floral splendour of Namaqualand. From 5–7, but up to 40, individuals may inhabit the same large outcrop, and these appear to be family units. This attractive species is endangered by illegal collecting. Gives birth to 1 or 2 large young in late summer.

WARREN'S GIRDLED LIZARD *Smaug warreni* 20–30cm

 This large, flattened girdled lizard is endemic to the Lebombo Mountains of the Swaziland-South Africa border. It has a *broad head* and *keeled dorsal scales in 34–42 girdles*. The body is golden brown, dirty cream on flanks and belly, with *6–8 rows of cream, black-edged spots* that may fuse to form irregular bands. The head is darker with light flecks. This lizard prefers rocky mountain slopes, favouring deep cracks in large boulders that are sheltered by trees. It is shy and difficult to approach. It eats insects, as well as snails and small lizards. Gives birth to 2–6 young in late summer.

GIANT GIRDLED LIZARD *Smaug giganteus* 20–35cm

 Due to its *large size* and *heavily spined body and tail*, this impressive girdled lizard is easily recognized. The back of the head has a fringe of *4 large occipital spines*. This species lives in long tunnels that it digs in rolling grassland. On sunny days it basks on termite nests. The common name 'sungazer' comes from this habit. It is long-lived and 1 or 2 young are born, but only every other year. It is threatened, as much of its range has been destroyed for maize farming. The surviving populations are also threatened by illegal collecting. **V**

BLUE-SPOTTED GIRDLED LIZARD
Ninurta coeruleopunctatus   13–16cm

A small, slender girdled lizard, easily identified by its *dark body with scattered enamel blue spots*. The dorsal scales are *small, and not separated by granules*. The flanks, snout and sides of the head may be rust-coloured, while breeding males often have greenish-yellow to orange throats. This species is restricted mainly to coastal rocks in the cool southern Cape, where it may form large colonies. The dark body allows it to absorb heat on cloudy days. This lizard digs a small tunnel in a soil-filled rock crack. Gives birth to 3 or 4 young in late summer.

GRACILE CRAG LIZARD *Hemicordylus capensis*   18–22cm

Although very similar to Blue-spotted Girdled Lizard, it *grows larger* and *lacks blue spots*. It has *long toes* and a *thin tail*, and runs easily over the vertical walls of large rock faces. The body is basically grey-black, although pale yellow vermiculations may be present on the head and back. This lizard lives on the rocky summits of the Cape Fold Mountains, and is shy and difficult to approach. A pair of adults often share the same retreat. The diet consists mainly of insects, particularly bees and wasps. Gives birth to 2 or 3 young in autumn.

CAPE CRAG LIZARD *Pseudocordylus microlepidotus* 25–30cm

 Sharing the Cape mountain summits with the Gracile Crag
Lizard (p.101), this impressive lizard lives in solitary splendour
in large rock cracks. It forages for food on flat rocks around
its retreat, eating large beetles and grasshoppers. With its
powerful jaws it can give a painful bite, and may kill and eat
other lizards. Although similar to girdled lizards, this species' *neck and flanks
are covered in granular scales* and the *tail is less spiny*. Breeding males have
brightly coloured flanks (orange in the east, yellow inland). Juveniles and
females are drabber, with grey-brown, blotched backs. Gives birth to 2–6,
usually 4, young in late summer.

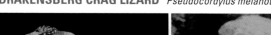

DRAKENSBERG CRAG LIZARD *Pseudocordylus melanotus* 20–26cm

Left: female; right: breeding male

The breeding males of this beautiful species are more colourful than those of Cape Crag Lizard. Although these 2 species are difficult to tell apart, their ranges do not overlap. The *large, powerful jaws* and *small scales on the flanks* identify it as a crag lizard. There is a *single row of 4–6 elongate temporal scales*. It is found in very dense colonies, and is the commonest lizard on the inhospitable rocky mountains of Lesotho. The insect diet is supplemented with flowers and berries during summer. This lizard spends winter in hibernation, deep in a rock crack. Gives birth to 1–6 young in summer.

NORTHERN CRAG LIZARD *Pseudocordylus transvaalensis* 22–30cm

A *very large* crag lizard, with a *double row of temporals on the side of the head*. It inhabits rock outcrops in montane grassland in isolated populations in Limpopo province. Breeding males are dark olive with 8 or 9 dark crossbars and bright yellow to orange flanks. Females are duller and lack the bright flanks. It occurs singly or in small colonies, with a dominant male and some females and young. Gives birth to 2–7 large young (up to 80mm) in midsummer. **NT**

Stu Neilsen

ATTENBOROUGH'S FLAT LIZARD
Platysaurus attenboroughi   18–21cm

 Flat lizards are unmistakable, with their flat bodies and beautiful male breeding colours. The back is covered in granular scales, while there are scattered spines on the legs. Females and juveniles in most species have black backs with 3 pale stripes. In this species, the breeding males develop electric blue, pale-spotted backs and blue, black-centred bellies, with coral-red tails. This species inhabits scattered colonies on granite rocks of the Richtersveld and Fish River Canyon. It shelters beneath a thin exfoliating rock flake. It lays 2 soft-shelled eggs in summer.

EASTERN FLAT LIZARD   *Platysaurus orientalis*   15–18cm

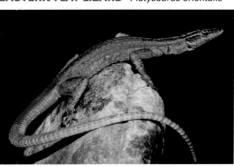

Very similar in appearance to Attenborough's Flat Lizard (above), but this species' adult males have dark green heads with 3 green stripes, green backs with scattered pale spots, and a brick red tail. The throat and belly are blue. The *lower eyelid*

 has a transparent window. It is found in the Mpumalanga Drakensberg and adjacent ranges, with a localized population in Sekhukhuniland. This lizard can be seen basking on rock faces at midday, but it is shy and quickly retreats into a nearby rock crack. Lays 2 eggs in a sun-warmed crack.

NATAL FLAT LIZARD *Platysaurus natalensis* 16–20cm

Although the breeding male has similar coloration to the Eastern Flat Lizard (p.104), this small species has an *opaque lower eyelid*. Males also have a darker blue belly, and a green gular region. It is restricted to rock outcrops in extreme north KwaZulu-Natal and adjacent regions. A large colony of these beautiful lizards foraging and basking on a rugged rock outcrop is a memorable sight. Lays 2 elongate eggs (8–11 x 14–22mm) in November within a sun-warmed rock crack. Numerous females may nest in the same crack.

COMMON FLAT LIZARD *Platysaurus intermedius* 19–25cm

A medium-sized flat lizard with an *opaque lower eyelid* and *fused supranasal and nasal scales*. The breeding male has similar coloration to the Eastern Flat Lizard (p.104), but has a *darker blue belly* and a *green gular region*. This species is widespread and common on low rock outcrops and koppies in northeastern Limpopo province. Males will bask in prominent positions and command exclusive territories, which they share with a number of females and juveniles. Lays 2 elongate eggs (11–18mm) in a sun-warmed rock crack. Favoured cracks may be used for many years and by numerous females.

WATERBERG FLAT LIZARD *Platysaurus minor* 14–18cm

Breeding male, showing back and bright belly colours

A small flat lizard with a *transparent 'window' in the lower eyelid*, and the *supranasal scale fused with the nasal*. The breeding male has a *dark brown back, red flanks and tail*, and *lime-yellow lips and throat*. This species is endemic to the greater Waterberg region of western Limpopo province. It prefers low-lying rock outcrops, often quite heavily shaded by trees, on the lower slopes of mountains. It occurs in small family groups, feeding on insects and occasionally fruit. Lays 2 eggs in a sun-warmed rock crack.

LEBOMBO FLAT LIZARD *Platysaurus lebomboensis* 17–21cm

In this unusual flat lizard the breeding male has a mainly *black back and belly*, and the *brick-red colour* of the tail extends onto the flanks. This species is restricted to the Lebombo Mountains of eastern Swaziland and adjacent regions, and is usually observed basking or foraging on rocky boulders or bedrock. Females may lay a number of 2-egg clutches during summer.

MONITORS (LEGUAANS) Family Varanidae

All monitors are similar in appearance, having long, flexible necks, well-developed limbs with strong claws, and a long tail that cannot be shed or regenerated. The head and body are covered in small, bead-like scales that lack osteoderms. The tongue is long and snake-like. About 40 species are found throughout Africa and Australasia, with only 2 reaching southern Africa. The family includes the world's largest lizards.

WATER MONITOR *Varanus niloticus*

120–220cm

This is Africa's largest lizard. It has an *elongate head* and the *flattened tail is much longer than the body* and aids swimming. The black-and-yellow barred juveniles are much brighter than the adults. This

lizard forages along river courses, searching for crabs and other aquatic organisms. Juveniles eat mainly insects and small frogs. Lays up to 60 eggs in a live termite nest, where they take 4–6 months to develop.

ROCK MONITOR *Varanus albigularis*

100–150cm

Similar to the Water Monitor (above), but *smaller*, with a *relatively shorter head and tail*. The *nasal region is swollen.* This lizard is a drab, mottled colour, usually well sullied with old skin and ticks. A great wanderer in arid, rocky habitats, it shelters in tunnels

and rock overhangs. It feeds mainly on large insects and millipedes, but also eats small tortoises and lizards. It usually escapes into trees or rock cracks, but will bite and lash with its tail if cornered. The bite can be strong and painful, but is not poisonous. Lays 8–50 eggs, usually in soft soil.

AGAMAS Family Agamidae

A large, diverse family found throughout Africa and Australasia. The 15 southern African species are all similar in appearance, being plump, short-bodied lizards with triangular heads and thin tails. The head is covered in small, irregular scales, and the big mouth has 2 fang-like teeth at the front of the upper jaw. Nonetheless, they are harmless. They are active, diurnal lizards, many of which feed predominantly on ants and termites. Males develop vivid breeding colours and defend territories. These lizards lay a relatively large clutch of soft-shelled eggs.

SOUTHERN ROCK AGAMA *Agama atra* 20–25cm

This agama is common on rock outcrops throughout the southern regions. It has an *enlarged occipital scale* on the crown, and a *small dorsal crest is present*, extending along the backbone onto the tail base. This species is usually found in

small colonies. The breeding male develops a *bright blue head* and displays from prominent rocks. Females and juveniles are drabber, and shy, and remain more hidden. Lays up to 18 eggs in summer, and sometimes lays another clutch in late summer.

ANCHIETA'S AGAMA *Agama anchietae* 15–20cm

This small agama is restricted to the western arid regions and prefers small rock outcrops, where it is usually found singly or in pairs. This species differs from Southern Rock Agama (above) in having *shorter toes, black-tipped scales on the soles of the feet*, and scattered, *enlarged spines on the back*. Lays 10–12 eggs in summer.

GROUND AGAMA *Agama aculeta*

15–22cm

Although widely distributed through the savannas and semi-arid regions of southern Africa, this is a shy species that does not form colonies. This agama has a relatively *large earhole* and the *throat markings form a central network. Enlarged spines on the back are arranged in regular rows.* The body is cryptically blotched in browns, although breeding males develop bluish heads. This lizard is most frequently seen browsing on a stream of ants passing to and from a nest, or basking in a low bush in the hot Kalahari. Lays 10–18 eggs in a hole in sandy soil.

SPINY AGAMA *Agama hispida*

15–20cm

Although similar in general appearance and habits to Ground Agama (above), this species can be distinguished by the *small earhole* and *irregular pale blotches on the dark throat.* The breeding male also has a *vivid, almost metallic yellow-green head and body*, and may display from a prominent boulder or bush. A pair may share a short tunnel dug into sandy soil at the base of a bush. This lizard runs rapidly when disturbed, and often uses rodents' tunnels as temporary shelters. Lays 7–11 eggs in spring in a hole in soft soil.

NAMIBIAN ROCK AGAMA *Agama planiceps* 22–30cm

This large, graceful agama is easily recognized by its *large hindlimbs*, *small head* and *long tail*. The juveniles and females have a grey-olive body with pale blotches and a bright orange

blotch behind the shoulders. The dark head has symmetrical lemon-yellow blotches. The breeding male's body develops a *metallic dull blue-purple sheen*, while the head, neck and throat are orange-red. The tail is olive-yellow at the base, becoming coral-red at the tip. This species forms dense colonies on granite outcrops in northern Namibia, where a few dominant males partition females and territory between them. The diet includes insects, leaves and seeds. Usually lays 6 or 7 eggs in a soil-filled rock crack, which hatch in 7–10 weeks.

SOUTHERN TREE AGAMA *Acanthocercus atricollis* 20–35cm

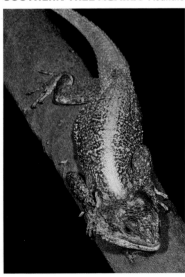

This agama has diagnostic *large black shoulder spots* and there is no *enlarged occipital scale* on the crown. Females and juveniles have cryptic, but attractive, lichen-coloured bodies, while breeding males develop bright ultramarine heads and orange tails. When threatened, it gapes widely, revealing a bright orange mouth lining, but it is harmless. It feeds mainly on flying insects, but will eat beetles and even small vertebrates. Common on trees in the eastern bushveld, this very large agama can be seen clinging to a tree trunk and nodding its head in display. During summer, the female lays 4–14 eggs in a hole she digs in the ground.

CHAMELEONS Family Chamaeleonidae

These unmistakable lizards are adapted for life in trees. They are mainly restricted to Africa and Madagascar. The compressed body and head are covered in small, granular scales. The large, turreted eyes can move independently. The toes are bound in uneven bundles and can clasp thin branches. The tail is prehensile, and cannot be shed or regenerated. Food is captured by the familiar telescopic tongue. At least 20 species, some unnamed, are found in the region.

FLAP-NECKED CHAMELEON *Chamaeleo dilepis* 20–24cm

The only chameleon found in the savannas of the northern regions. It is characterized by *large occipital skin flaps* behind the head and a *crest of small, white scales on the throat and belly.* The body colour may vary from green to pale yellow through to brown. This chameleon gapes widely in defence, revealing the orange mouth lining, and flattens the body while rocking from side to side. It will bite, but is not poisonous. The female digs a long tunnel and lays up to 57 small eggs that may take up to 9 months to develop.

NAMAQUA CHAMELEON *Chamaeleo namaquensis* 18–22cm

This is the largest local chameleon species. This terrestrial chameleon inhabits some of the hottest and most desolate regions. It is ungainly, with a *large head, short tail,* and a *series of 12–14 knob-like tubercles along the back.* It eats large numbers of grasshoppers and beetles, and will also eat small lizards and even snakes. This chameleon may even forage along the high tide line. A nasal gland allows it to get rid of excess salt. On hot days it climbs into low bushes, or onto rocks, to cool in any breeze. Lays 2 or 3 clutches of 6–22 eggs in a burrow in sand.

CAPE DWARF CHAMELEON *Bradypodion pumilum* 13–16cm

Krystal Tolley

A beautiful and common resident of gardens in the southwestern Cape. The leaf green body usually has an orange-red lateral strip. The throat region is pale green to yellow, with a *crest of elongate scales that do not overlap*. The *tail is longer than the body*. This species is less antisocial than many other chameleons, and up to 5 or 6 may be found in a single bush. Like all dwarf chameleons, it gives birth to 6–10 young while clinging to a branch. The young are in sticky sacs that adhere to the leaves; they then struggle till they break through the membranes and are free. It may have 2 or 3 litters each year. **V**

SWARTBERG DWARF CHAMELEON
Bradypodion atromontanum 11–13cm

Werner Conradie

A *small chameleon with a tail shorter than the body*. The *casque is not prominent* and there are at least *2 pale bluish gular grooves*. This chameleon is mottled green, with an orange eye and black band that runs from the eye to the neck, as well as onto the mid-body in display. Females and juveniles are more subdued in colour. This species inhabits mountain fynbos and is endemic to the Swartberg. Breeding is poorly known, but is probably similar to other dwarf chameleons.

SOUTHERN DWARF CHAMELEON *Bradypodion ventrale* 12–14cm

This *large* dwarf chameleon has a curious distribution, with isolated colonies in the Western and Eastern Cape. It has a *prominent casque* on the back of the head, and a *throat crest of large, overlapping, scaly flaps*. The *tail is shorter than the body* in both sexes. This species inhabits dense thicket in the east and low coastal scrub in the west. Its camouflage colours make it difficult to see during the day, but it turns grey-white at night and can easily be found with a torch. It adapts well to urban gardens. It has 1 or 2 litters of up to 22 young each summer.

SMITH'S DWARF CHAMELEON
Bradypodion taeniabronchum

8–11cm

Krystal Tolley

This *very small* species is easily distinguished by the *black throat grooves*, which are prominent when the throat is inflated in threat. Adults are usually lichen-coloured, although males may be rust-red with maroon throat grooves. It is Endangered and is threatened by habitat destruction. It has a very restricted distribution, being known only from a few small mountain ranges in the Eastern Cape. It lives in protea bushes and low fynbos, feeding on insects attracted by the flowers. Gives birth to up to 13 tiny young in summer. **E**

SETARO'S DWARF CHAMELEON *Bradypodion setaroi* 9–12cm

Krystal Tolley

This is a *small* species that lives in low coastal dune forest in northern Zululand, but that has adapted well to urban gardens. The *casque is narrow and well developed*, but the *throat crest is reduced*. The *tail is longer than the body* in males, but shorter in females. The gular region is *light green* with *white throat grooves*. Gives birth to a number of small litters of 6–8 minute young during summer.

NATAL MIDLANDS DWARF CHAMELEON
Bradypodion thamnobates 15–18cm

Krystal Tolley

This is one of the largest and most attractive dwarf chameleons, with a *large, recurved casque* and a *throat crest of long, overlapping scaly flaps*. A *pronounced dorsal crest* extends along the back and onto the tail. Males in display are dark blue-green with a cream or red-brown lateral patch. The cranial crests become horn-coloured. Like most other chameleons, it is very asocial and will threaten and chase off other specimens entering its territory. Gives birth to 8–20 young, which grow quickly, reaching maturity in a year. **V**

KNYSNA DWARF CHAMELEON · *Bradypodion damaranum* · 16–19cm

This *large* dwarf chameleon has an *enlarged, rounded casque* and a *throat crest of white, overlapping scaly flaps*. The *dorsal crest extends along the back and tail*, which is *much longer than the body*. Males in display are *bright green* with a large, smooth, *lemon yellow patch at the armpit*. The skin between the cranial crests becomes *pinkish-cream*. It climbs high in the canopy of the southern Cape forests, but also uses low bushes along streams and adapts well to gardens. Gives birth to several litters of 6–20 young each summer.

WEST COAST DWARF CHAMELEON
Bradypodion occidentale · 15–17cm

Krystal Tolley

Another *large* dwarf chameleon with a *large, recurved casque* and *long, deep gular grooves* that extend onto the neck. The skin in the grooves may vary from *bright orange-red to black*. The gular crest is *well developed with large, overlapping flaps*. This species is usually lichen-coloured, but in display the male may develop bright blue tubercles on the head and body. It inhabits strandveld along the West Coast, where it can be very common, feeding on insects attracted by the coastal flowers. Gives birth to up to 20 young in summer.

GECKOS Family Gekkonidae

Widely distributed throughout the world, this is the most diverse lizard family in southern Africa, with over 100 species. Most species have immovable eyelids, which are wiped clean with the tongue. Many have complicated toes, with claws and expanded tips (scansors) that have specialized scales covered with minute hairs. These allow them to climb smooth vertical surfaces. Most are nocturnal, and have large eyes with complicated pupils that open fully at night. All local species lay 1 or 2 hard-shelled eggs.

AFRICAN FLAT GECKO *Afroedura africana*   10–12cm

This gecko has an elongate, *flattened body* with *3 pairs of scansors* beneath the *dilated, clawed toe-tips*. The original *tail is segmented* and *slightly longer than the body*. Males have *13–15 preanal pores*. The back is pale buff with 5 or 6 wavy, dark brown bands that may break into blotches. This species lives under thin rock flakes in scattered populations in central Namibia.

LIMPOPO FLAT GECKO *Afroedura transvaalica*   10–12cm

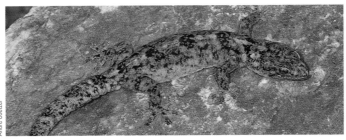

André Coetzer

Similar to the African Flat Gecko (above), but with only *2 pairs of scansors* on each toe-tip and with a *browner body*. It is found in isolated populations on rock outcrops and also on baobab trunks. Despite the scientific name, it is found mainly in Zimbabwe. It is communal, and up to 20 individuals may live in the same crack.

TEMBU FLAT GECKO *Afroedura tembulica* 10–12cm

This species has a *flattened body* with *3 pairs of scansors* beneath the *dilated, clawed toe-tips*. The original *tail is segmented* and *slightly longer than the body*. Males have *6–9 preanal pores*. The back is yellowish-brown with reticulated darker brown markings and scattered pale spots. This gecko inhabits cracks in scattered boulders in montane grassland around Queenstown in the Eastern Cape.

MARIPI FLAT GECKO *Afroedura maripi* 9–11cm

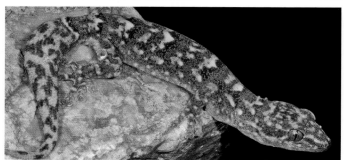

This species has a *flattened body* with *2 pairs of scansors* beneath the *dilated, clawed toe-tips*. The original *tail is not segmented*. There is a *single internasal granule*, and males have *11–13 preanal pores*. The back is dark brown with scattered pale blotches, which are largest along the backbone. The tail has about 10 black bands. This species is endemic to Marieskop in the eastern escarpment. Lays 2 eggs at a time during August–October.

GECKOS

HAWEQUA FLAT GECKO *Afroedura hawequensis*   12–15cm

 A *very large* and attractive flat gecko with a stout body and *3 pairs of scansors under all toes*, except the first. Males have *30–32 preanal pores* in a curved row. The *original tail is segmented;* the regenerated tail is fat and leaf-like. It lives in narrow cracks in well-shaded sandstone boulders in the Hawequa Mountains of the southwestern Cape. Up to 5 individuals may share the same retreat. Lays 2 large eggs in early summer. **NT**

KAROO FLAT GECKO *Afroedura karroica*   10–12cm

 This *medium-sized* gecko has *3 pairs of scansors*, a *segmented tail*, and *no enlarged chin shields*. Males have *6–8 preanal pores*. Found singly, or in pairs, in fine rock cracks, this species lives on large sandstone outcrops or boulders in arid montane grassland in the Eastern Cape. Preferred retreats are weathered sandstone flakes that catch the evening sun and are protected from seeping water. This gecko emerges in the early evening to forage on rock faces for ants and small beetles. Lays 2 hard-shelled eggs beneath a sun-warmed flake, and communal nest sites may contain hundreds of old and fresh eggs.

MARLEY'S FLAT GECKO *Afroedura marleyi* 7–9cm

A *small* flat gecko with a *thin body* and *2 pairs of scansors under toes*. Males have *10–14 preanal pores*. The *original tail is not segmented*, and the *dorsal scales are faintly keeled*. The most terrestrial of all flat geckos, and often found singly or in pairs under bark, in dead aloe stems, or under rock slabs. Lays 2 very small eggs (6–8mm dia.) frequently during summer.

AMATOLA FLAT GECKO *Afroedura amatolica* 10–12cm

Endemic to the Amatola Mountains of the Eastern Cape, this flat gecko has *3 pairs of scansors and* a *segmented tail*. Males have *10–12 preanal pores*. This species forms small colonies where up to 10 geckos can use the same rock crack on the granite outcrop. It hibernates

in deep rock fissures to avoid winter snow that may cover the mountains. Lays 2 hard-shelled eggs beneath a sun-warmed flake of rock, and communal nest sites contain many old and fresh eggs.

TROPICAL HOUSE GECKO *Hemidactylus mabouia* 12–15cm

This gecko is easily distinguished by its *large, flared toe-tips* that have *paired scansors* and a *large, retractile claw.* There are *10–18 irregular rows of weakly keeled tubercles on the back* and *22–40 preanal pores.* The body is pale grey with 4 or 5

wavy, dark crossbars that fade in the light. Males are territorial and will fight each other. Once restricted to the lowveld and KwaZulu-Natal, this species is now rapidly expanding its range throughout South Africa. It is normally found on trees, where it shelters under bark or in hollow logs, but adapts easily to houses, where it feeds on moths attracted to lights. Communal eggs sites may contain up to 60 eggs.

FLAT-HEADED HOUSE GECKO
Hemidactylus platycephalus 15–20cm

This arboreal gecko is similar to the Tropical House Gecko (above), but grows *larger,* and has *more conspicuous crossbars on the body* and *45–57 preanal pores.* It lives in large hollow trees, but regularly climbs on house walls. It occurs from central Mozambique and adjacent eastern Zimbabwe, northwards into coastal East Africa.

STRIPED LEAF-TOED GECKO *Goggia lineata* 4–5cm

This *tiny, delicate* gecko is one of the smallest lizards in the region. It often has a series of *conspicuous dark grey stripes* on the pale grey back, but these may be broken into irregular scallops. The *toe-tips are flared, with a single large pair of scansors.* This gecko is terrestrial and nocturnal, sheltering under rubble or among dead scrub, particularly dried succulents. It may live under the bark of dead trees along dry river courses. The diet is composed of small insects, particularly termites. Lays 2 small, hard-shelled eggs in a moist, warm spot.

SMALL-SCALED LEAF-TOED GECKO *Goggia microlepidota* 9–13cm

Sebastian Kirchhof

A large, attractive, but secretive gecko with *paired, leaf-shaped scansors under each toe-tip.* The back is covered in *minute, flattened scales*, from which it gets its name. The flat body is slate-grey with a blackish, reticulate pattern. This species is restricted to the western Cape Fold Mountains from the Cederberg to Ceres. Here it lives in large rock cracks in the sandstone summit outcrops in mountain fynbos. It prefers large, shaded cracks, and is usually solitary.

HEWITT'S LEAF-TOED GECKO *Goggia hewitti*

4–5cm

This tiny, delicate gecko's *toe-tips are flared, with a single large pair of scansors.* The back is light tan-brown with 7 irregular dark brown bars that may become reticulate or fragment into pale-centred scallops. It is rock-living and nocturnal, sheltering under boulders and in rock cracks and inhabiting low sandstone outcrops in the eastern Cape Fold Mountains.

SWARTBERG LEAF-TOED GECKO
Ramigecko swartbergensis

8–9cm

This *large*, flattened gecko has *large, flared toe-tips*, each with *paired scansors and a well-developed claw.* There are *no preanal pores.* The back has *enlarged smooth tubercles surrounded by granules.* The body is greyish-brown mottled with tans and creams, and with vague dark blotches. This species is endemic to the Swartberg of the inner Cape Fold Mountains, where it inhabits deep rock cracks on the summit sandstones. Docile, it relies on immobility and camouflage to avoid detection.

PÉRINGUEY'S LEAF-TOED GECKO *Cryptactites peringueyi* 4–5cm

Werner Conradie

This very small gecko has *paired leaf-shaped scansors* under the toe-tips, a *sharp snout* and *numerous enlarged tubercles* on the back. The red-brown body may have a series of thin dark stripes. It is unique among local lizards, as it lives in coastal and estuarine habitats. For a long time this species was thought extinct, but was rediscovered in 1992 in the Kromme estuary in the Eastern Cape. It is considered Critically Endangered. It is a small, cryptic, nocturnal gecko, living at the edge of salt marshes or at the strand line in rotting logs or matted vegetation at the base of restio clumps. The latter form a favoured nesting place, where clutches of 2 minute, hard-shelled eggs are laid throughout summer. **CE**

MARBLED LEAF-TOED GECKO *Afrogecko porphyreus* 8–9cm

This gecko's feet are similar to those of Péringuey's Leaf-toed Gecko (above), and the tail is *round, unsegmented,* and *longer than the body*. The *back is smooth* and marbled grey in colour,

sometime with a pale dorsal stripe. This species is found throughout the southern Cape coastal regions. It is adaptable, living happily under tree bark, in rock cracks or even in suburban houses. It is not aggressive, and as many as 24 individuals may share the same retreat. Communal eggs sites, under tree bark or a suitable stone on sandy soil, may contain numerous new and old eggs.

CAPE DWARF DAY GECKO *Lygodactylus capensis* 6–7cm

A delightful dwarf day gecko that is often seen running on trees or garden walls. It has a *rudimentary inner toe*, while the other toes have dilated tips, with *large and paired oblique scansors*. The *mental has lateral clefts*. The grey-brown body has a dark streak from the snout to the shoulder. The throat is usually stippled with grey and the belly is cream. It feeds almost exclusively on ants and termites. If disturbed, this gecko may freeze or dash behind cover. It is often found in gardens, and has been translocated to many towns outside its natural range. Breeding is continuous and communal egg sites are common.

STEVENSON'S DWARF DAY GECKO
Lygodactylus stevensoni 6–7cm

This stout dwarf day gecko has a *rudimentary inner toe*, while the other toes have dilated tips, with *large and paired oblique scansors*. It differs from Cape Dwarf Day Gecko (above) in having a *more pointed snout,* a *blue-grey body* with

scattered *black spots*, and *dark chevrons* on the throat. This species is mainly rock-living, although it may shelter under dead bark, or run on the trunks of large fig trees. It is restricted to well-wooded, rock outcrops along the central Limpopo Valley.

OCELLATED DWARF DAY GECKO *Lygodactylus ocellatus* 5–7cm

This species *has a rudimentary inner toe*, while the other toes have *dilated tips* with *large claws* and *paired oblique scansors*. The *mental lacks lateral clefts*. The light tan body has numerous scattered *pale-centred dark spots*. This gecko is endemic to Mpumalanga and southeastern Limpopo, where it lives among rocks and stones on exposed hillsides.

MAKGABENG DWARF DAY GECKO
Lygodactylus montiscaeruli 6–8cm

This small gecko *has a rudimentary inner toe*, while the other toes have *dilated tips* with *large claws* and *paired oblique scansors*. The *mental lacks lateral clefts*. This species differs from Ocellated Dwarf Day Gecko (above) in being *larger* and having different coloration. The grey-brown body has a characteristic row of 4 or 5 dorsolateral black spots that may extend on to the tail. This gecko is endemic to the Makgabeng Hills and Blouberg in Limpopo province. It lives mainly on rocks but may also climb trees.

NAMAQUA DAY GECKO *Rhoptropella ocellata* 6–7cm

This small, drab day gecko can easily be confused with dwarf day geckos due to its *small inner toe*. However, it has a *stouter build* and the *flared toe-tips have 7 or 8 undivided scansors* and *no claw*. The *brown body* has numerous *small dark and pale spots*. This species occurs in the succulent, semi-arid wastes of Namaqualand. It prefers well-vegetated rocky hillsides, where it runs and hops over boulders and may climb into succulent bushes. The diet consists of small insects. Lays a number of clutches of 2 small, hard-shelled eggs during summer.

FESTIVE GECKO *Narudasia festiva* 5–6cm

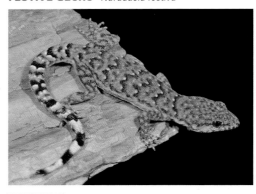

This *very small*, diurnal, flattened gecko is easily distinguished by the *slender, clawed toes* that *lack flared tips or adhesive scansors*. The brown body has numerous pale and dark blotches that may coalesce into irregular crossbars. The *original tail is bright yellow-orange*, but uniform

grey when regenerated. This gecko forages on rocks in the western arid regions but is restricted to southern Namibia. It is a very agile species, and catches ants and small flies on the rock walls and boulders of the mountains. Lays 2 hard-shelled eggs in a rock crack.

COMMON BARKING GECKO *Ptenopus garrulus* 6–8cm

Barking geckos differ from other local geckos in having *movable upper eyelids* and *short toes that lack scansors*, but *have a scaly fringe* to aid digging. In this small species, the body colour varies from reddish-brown to greyish-yellow, either finely speckled or with black crossbars. The male has an *orange or yellow throat*. It digs branching tunnels in firm sand at the base of bushes. Males call (*'ceek, ceek, ceek...'*) from the entrance of the burrow to attract mates. Their clicking chorus can be deafening during summer sunsets in the western arid regions. Lays several clutches of 2 (sometimes 1) hard-shelled eggs during summer.

CARP'S BARKING GECKO *Ptenopus carpi* 9–12cm

A slender barking gecko that has large, *bulging eyes, swollen nostrils*, and *minute body scales*. The *toes are only weakly fringed*. The body is creamy white with fine orange-brown speckles. There are 3–5 dark brown crossbars on the back and 5–9 on the tail. Adult males have sulphur-yellow throats. These geckos prefer compact sands in gravel plains of coastal northern Namibia, and are active late on cold, foggy nights.

WAHLBERG'S VELVET GECKO *Homopholis wahlbergii* 14–20cm

This *large arboreal* gecko's toe pads are expanded with *8–12 unpaired, chevron-shaped scansors* and *small claws*. The back is covered in *small, overlapping scales*, and *lacks enlarged tubercles*. Males have a *pair of enlarged preanal*

scales with pores. The body is light mottled grey with about 6 or 7 large pale spots and vague dark crossbars. The belly is usually a dirty cream colour, sometimes with dark flecks. This species shelters beneath bark or in holes in baobab trees. It may even use old swallow nests or rock cracks, and also climbs on houses. It eats large insects, including grasshoppers, cockroaches, beetles and termites. It lays a pair of large, white eggs in a rock crack or under bark.

ARNOLD'S VELVET GECKO *Homopholis arnoldi* 18–23cm

Very similar to Wahlberg's Velvet Gecko (above), with which it has long been confused. It grows slightly larger, but also differs in coloration, with most specimens having *broad black dorsolateral stripes*, sometimes separated by pale blotches and/or connected with black crossbars. It occurs mainly north of the Limpopo River, from eastern Botswana to Mozambique.

GIAGNT GROUND GECKO *Chondrodactylus angulifer* 13–16cm

Top: male (back) and female (front); above: male from Namib Desert
(left), foot without scansors (right)

A large terrestrial gecko with a stout, *cylindrical body*. The big
head has a *short snout and large eyes*. The short toes *lack
scansors*. The back has *scattered keeled tubercles* and the *tail is
segmented, ringed with enlarged tubercles* and is *shorter than
the body*. The back colour is usually pale orange to red-brown,
sometimes with pale, dark-edged chevrons. The belly is pink-white. This species
inhabits gravel plains and sandy flats in the Namib Desert and Karoo. Nocturnal,
it emerges from its burrow at night to feed on insects and other small geckos.
When alarmed, it walks stiff-legged with the tail arched, scorpion-like, over the
back. It may bite, but is harmless.

BIBRON'S GECKO *Chondrodactylus bibronii*   15–19cm

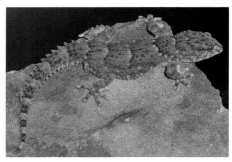

This species and Turner's Gecko (below) are the most familiar and widespread of the region's geckos. The back has numerous *enlarged, conical tubercles* with a *distinct longitudinal keel*. It is a large, *stout-bodied* gecko, with a *triangular head* and *powerful jaws*. The tail is segmented with *regular whorls of spiny scales*. The grey

to brown back has numerous scattered white spots, and 4 or 5 indistinct dark crossbars, which are often more distinct in juveniles. It lives in rock cracks, under tree bark and in houses, and forms large colonies. Pugnacious, they are ever willing to give a painful bite.

TURNER'S GECKO *Chondrodactylus turneri*   15–19cm

This species is easily confused with Bibron's Gecko (above), but may have smoother tubercles on the back, and the *scales bordering the mental are larger*. This species is restricted to the arid western regions, and is only found on large rock outcrops. It shelters in rock cracks, but is less gregarious and usually found singly or in pairs. Lays 2 or 3 clutches of eggs in sand in a rock crack in spring and summer. The young hatch in 60–80 days.

KALAHARI GROUND GECKO *Colopus wahlbergii* 9–12cm

A small terrestrial gecko of the central Kalahari Desert. It has a *cylindrical body* covered in *smooth granules*. The toe-tips are only slightly expanded, with just *2 undivided scansors and no claws* (except on the hindfeet of females). There are *no preanal pores*. The back is light orange-brown with a series of large pale-centred dark spots along the backbone. The belly is chalky white. This gecko is usually found singly in a short burrow at the base of a grass tussock.

HAACKE'S GECKO *Pachydactylus haackei* 12–16cm

The genus *Pachydactylus* is the most diverse in the region, containing over 50 species. They are nocturnal and the long toes have swollen tips, with undivided scansors, and rudimentary claws. This *large, stout* species has a rough, but *delicate skin* that tears easily if it is grabbed. This is a defence mechanism and, like a lost tail, the skin can be regenerated quickly. There are *10 or 11 scansors* under the middle toe, and the *fat tail lacks lateral spines*. The body may be pink-grey with a series of 6 or 7 irregular bands. This gecko lives in rock cracks on large outcrops in the Richtersveld and southern Namibia.

VAN SON'S GECKO *Pachydactylus vansoni*   9–12cm

This gecko's *cylindrical body* has *rows of keeled tubercles*, and the *toes have 4–6 scansors*. The *tail is slightly longer than the body*. The body is brown with *5–8 narrow, white, black-edged stripes*. This is a terrestrial species, found from near sea level in Maputoland to the top of the Soutpansberg in Limpopo province. It is usually found singly under a stone on soil in grassland. Lays a number of egg clutches during the summer months.

CAPE GECKO *Pachydactylus capensis*   9–14cm

This terrestrial gecko has a *robust body* with *16–24 rows of keeled tubercles*. The *tail is slightly longer than the body*, and the toe-tips have *4–6 scansors*. The body is pale tan-brown, flecked with small black and white spots. This gecko is common in the central arid region, living in a small burrow under calcrete boulders or dead logs. Small insects, particularly termites, form the main diet. Lays clutches of 2 hard-shelled eggs throughout summer.

WEBER'S GECKO *Pachydactylus weberi*   9–10cm

This small, flattened gecko has numerous *rows of small tubercles* on the back and on the hindlimbs. These may be golden in colour, giving a *speckled, almost jewelled appearance*. The juvenile is golden-brown with

a *white* collar and *3 or 4 cream, dark-edged crossbars* on the body. The tail has bright alternating *black and white bands*. The body crossbars fade in the adult, but the banded tail is retained, although the regenerated tail is plain grey-brown. This gecko is very common in suitable habitat, but is rarely seen. Usually only a single individual, occasionally a pair, inhabit a crack.

AUGRABIES GECKO *Pachydactylus atorquatus*   8–11cm

This beautiful gecko has a cylindrical body with *14 rows of strongly keeled tubercles*. The *tail is slightly longer than the body*, and the toe-tips have *4 or 5 scansors*. It *lacks a white collar* and the body and tail are *uniform purplish-brown*, with tubercles pale-tipped, giving a speckled appearance. The *upper lip is bright white*. It inhabits boulder crevices and caves in the granite rocks bordering the Orange River.

AUSTEN'S GECKO *Pachydactylus austeni* 7–9cm

The body is cylindrical, the snout short, and the *large eyes have a conspicuous white or bright yellow eyelid*. The body scales are *smooth and granular*. There are only *3 or 4 scansors* beneath the toe-tips. Body colour is varied, ranging from pale grey to dark brown, with scattered dark and pale spots that may fuse to form irregular bars. This gecko can be found under stones and debris in the sparsely vegetated coastal dunes of the Western Cape. It lives in a small burrow dug in sand, and emerges at night to forage for small insects.

SPECKLED GECKO *Pachydactylus punctatus* 6–8cm

This beautiful, gentle gecko *lacks enlarged tubercles* on the back and has only *3 or 4 scansors* under the toe-tips. The tail is usually light orange in colour, sometimes with golden scale tips. The back is light brown with irregular darker blotches and

scattered pale spots. This species is terrestrial and lives on sandy soils from the Limpopo valley north to Tanzania. This small gecko lives in burrows, and is usually found under stones or dead longs on sand.

SPOTTED GECKO *Pachydactylus maculatus* 6–9cm

This terrestrial gecko has a *fat body* with rounded snout, and *only small tubercles on the back*. The body is always pale grey with *4 rows of black spots*, which may be separated by white interspaces and fuse to form irregular stripes. A *black eye-stripe* passes from the snout to the back of the head. It is the commonest terrestrial gecko in the Eastern Cape, becoming rarer elsewhere. It lives under debris, in rotting logs or old termite nests. A favorite retreat is an empty giant land snail shell. Small insects and spiders form the main diet. Lays 3 or 4 clutches of 2 hard-shelled eggs in summer.

BARNARD'S GECKO *Pachydactylus barnardi* 9–11cm

Previously confused with the Rough-scaled Gecko (p.137), this small, boldly patterned gecko has irregular rows of *enlarged and keeled tubercles* on the body, with numerous *spiny tubercles* on the *fat tail*. There are *5 scansors* beneath

the toe-tips. The head has a prominent dark chocolate band, bordered with white, from the snout through the eye and on to the neck. There are 5 paired chocolate-brown blotches on the body and 6–8 bands on the tail. This gecko is terrestrial, living under stones and thick vegetation mats on sandy soils in Little Namaqualand. Hatchlings appear in autumn.

OCELLATED GECKO *Pachydactylus geitje* 6–8cm

This is another small gecko with a confusing array of colour patterns. The grey-brown to dark brown body usually has small, scattered, *dark-edged pale spots*, although these may fade in mountain populations. The cylindrical body has smooth scales, and there are *4 or 5 scansors* under the toe-tips. In the moister, western regions this gecko is terrestrial, hiding among debris and under stones. Inland and further east it is restricted to mountains and is found more often in rock cracks. When at rest, it curls its fat tail around itself like a contented cat.

MARICO GECKO *Pachydactylus mariquensis* 8–10cm

A small, *slender, thin-legged gecko* with a *short snout* and *smooth body scales*. As with most terrestrial species, it has only *3 or 4 scansors* under the toe-tips. The cylindrical, unsegmented tail is slightly shorter than the body. The grey to pinkish-buff back has 5 or 6 wavy, reddish-brown, dark-edged crossbars. A pale dorsal stripe may be present. This species is found throughout the southwestern arid region, with scattered populations in the Eastern Cape. It spends the day sheltering in a burrow in sandy soil, from which it emerges in the evening to hunt small insects.

WEB-FOOTED GECKO *Pachydactylus rangei*

10–12cm

Easily recognized by its large, *jewel-like eyes*, this beautiful and bizarre gecko lives in the windblown sands of the Namib Desert. The large, *flat head* has *swollen nostrils*, and all the *toes are webbed and lack scansors*. The *tail is short, cylindrical and unsegmented*. The semi-transparent body is fleshy pink with dark reticulations, and there is a dark brown band across the snout. This gecko spends the day in a tunnel dug in fine sand, and emerges to feed on crickets and spiders at dusk. It walks with a stiff-legged gait, and wipes windblown sand from its eyes with its large tongue. Lays clutches of 2 large, hard-shelled eggs from November to March. **CE**

ROUGH-SCALED GECKO *Pachydactylus rugosus*

9–10cm

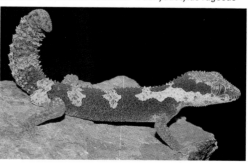

This small, round-bodied gecko is easily recognized by its *very rough, almost spiny skin*. The olive-green-brown back has *4 creamy, wavy crossbars*. There is often a *white stripe on the side of the head*. This species is restricted to the

western arid regions, where it lives under tree bark or among dead twigs and debris along dry river courses. When threatened, it behaves like a scorpion, standing stiff-legged and arching its banded tail high over its back. It also gapes to reveal its pink mouth lining.

NAMIB DAY GECKO *Rhoptropus afer*   8–10cm

This is the commonest of a group of diurnal geckos of the arid Namib region that have *long legs and toes*, with a *reduced inner toe*. The *toe-tips are flared with undivided scansors.* There are *5 or*

6 scansors under the middle toe. This gecko favours broken ground, where it darts rapidly on and between boulders. The back has *small, smooth, rounded scales*, and the grey, dappled body is perfectly camouflaged. However, the lower surfaces of the legs, tail and throat are bright yellow. Individuals 'flag' each other by lifting the tail to reveal the bright yellow colour. If there is a cooling breeze, it climbs onto rocks and lifts its body high. Ants and small beetles form the main diet. Lays 2 hard-shelled eggs in a rock crack.

BRADFIELD'S DAY GECKO *Rhoptropus bradfieldi*   10–13cm

This large day gecko differs from Namib Day Gecko (above) in being *larger*, having 11 *scansors* under the middle toe, and a *tail slightly longer than the body*. The sooty brown to blackish body has faint crossbars, and the belly is bluish-slate; it turns blackish during the day. This gecko lives in semi-desert in central Namibia, where it hangs from vertical, shaded rock faces looking for food.

BOULTON'S DAY GECKO *Rhoptropus boultoni*

12–15cm

The largest day gecko, it has a stocky body and longish toes, with 13 scansors under each toe-tip. The tail is *flattened, thick and segmented* at its base, and *slightly longer than the body*. The back is dark sooty grey to olive-brown with large scattered

maroon to dull red blotches. This gecko prefers rocky desert, from Damaraland into southern Angola. It forages on vertical granite boulders and even baobab trees, catching insects and ants. The males are aggressive and defend territories.

BARNARD'S DAY GECKO *Rhoptropus barnardi*

6–8cm

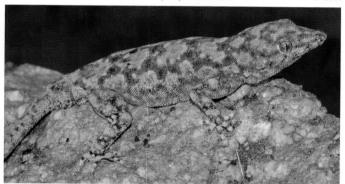

This small day gecko differs from Boulton's Day Gecko (above) in having *8 scansors* under the middle toe and *slightly keeled scales on the back*. The light grey to pink-brown body has scattered light and dark spots that may form rows. This gecko lives in semi-desert in northern Namibia, in regions of higher rainfall, preferring small rock outcrops and ridges. Lays clutches of 2 eggs in a rock crack in winter, and communal sites may contain over 200 old and new eggs.

WORM LIZARDS Family Amphisbaenidae

For a long time these unusual reptiles were not considered to be lizards. They are the most specialized burrowing reptiles, capable of driving tunnels through compact soils. They spend all their lives underground, feeding on insect larvae and other invertebrates. All local species lack limbs, eyes, or external ear openings. The scales of the cylindrical body are arranged in rings (annuli), giving them an appearance similar to worms (hence the common name). The head often has a specialized cutting edge for digging. They may lay eggs or give birth to young, and only about 12 species are found in the northern parts of the region.

KALAHARI ROUND-HEADED WORM LIZARD
Zygaspis quadrifrons

16–20cm

This small worm lizard has a *rounded head* that *lacks a cutting edge*, and has *198–242 body annuli*. The body is uniformly purple-brown above, with a lighter belly. This worm lizard inhabits sandy scrub and bushveld in the northern regions, where it feeds on small insects and their larvae, particularly termites.

VAN DAM'S ROUND-HEADED WORM LIZARD
Zygaspis vandami

16–20cm

A small worm lizard very similar in biology and appearance to the Kalahari Round-headed Worm Lizard (above). It has fewer body annuli (181–211) and *lacks a preocular* (which is fused with the prefrontals). The body is uniform purple-brown above, with a lighter belly and *white patches on the chin and cloacal region*. This species inhabits mesic savanna and coastal scrub on alluvial sands in the lowveld and Zululand coastal region.

CAPE SPADE-SNOUTED WORM LIZARD
Monopelis capensis

25–36cm

Werner Conradie

This large, *uniformly pink* worm lizard has a large *spade-shaped snout*, with a horizontal cutting edge that is used to dig deep tunnels. On the belly, just behind the throat, are *4–6 enlarged, elongate scales*. This worm lizard digs in the deep, red sands of the southern Kalahari, extending into the Limpopo River valley. It is only seen during excavations, or when floods push it to the surface. Gives birth to 1–3 young in late summer.

BLUNT-TAILED WORM LIZARD *Dalophia pistillum*

35–58cm

A *very large* worm lizard. Its *large, spade-shaped snout* has a horizontal cutting edge that is used to dig deep tunnels. On the belly, just behind the throat, are *6 enlarged, elongate scales*. The long *tail*

ends in a blunt callous. It is uniformly pink, with a few light grey flecks on the back. This worm lizard digs in the deep sands of the Kalahari, extending through Zimbabwe to central Mozambique. It builds long burrows and hunts beetle larvae and other insects. Lays 3 or 4 eggs in summer.

CROCODILES Order Crocodylia

These remnants of the dinosaur's rule are now endangered throughout the world. All are aquatic and the 27 species are distributed throughout the tropical regions. Recent studies have shown that the 3 African crocodiles previously recognized contained cryptic species. There are now at least 6 African species in 3 genera, of which only the Nile Crocodile reaches southern Africa.

NILE CROCODILE *Crocodylus niloticus* 250–550cm

One of the largest living crocodiles, it may exceed *1,000kg* in weight and nearly *6m* in length. As in birds, the eye has an *extra eyelid* that sweeps away dirt. The eyes and *valved nostrils* are placed high on the head. The *hindfeet are webbed* and the long tail, which cannot be shed, has *2 raised dorsal keels*. Adults are a dull olive with a yellow or cream belly. Hatchlings are brighter, with irregular black markings and a straw-yellow belly. Hatchlings and subadults live in marshes and backwaters, and feed mainly on insects and frogs. Adults move to more open water holes and dams, where they ambush mammals and birds. Fish, particularly catfish, also form an important component of the diet. Viable populations are now restricted to game reserves in the northern and eastern regions. Crocodiles are attentive parents, and the female digs a nest hole on a sandbank, within which she lays 16–80 oval, hard-shelled eggs. Incubated by the sun, they hatch in about 85 days. The sex of the hatchlings depends on the incubation temperature; females are produced at low temperatures (26–30°C) and males at higher temperatures (31–34°C). The parents protect the nest during development, and will also assist the hatchlings from the nest and carry them to water. Growth is slow, and maturity occurs in 12–15 years at 2–3m. **V**

CHELONIANS Order Testudines
SIDE-NECKED TERRAPINS Family Pelomedusidae

Primitive chelonians that move their neck sideways so that one eye is still visible when the head is withdrawn. They are restricted to the southern continents.

SERRATED HINGED TERRAPIN *Pelusios sinuatus* 30–45cm

A large freshwater terrapin that has a *hard, domed shell* with a distinct *hinge at the front of the plastron*. This closes to protect the head. The rear of the shell is *serrated* and there are *keels along the backbone*, particularly in juveniles. The shell is black, except

for a yellow, angular-edged blotch in the centre of the belly. The thick, heavy shell protects it from crocodiles. This species is common in large rivers and pans in the eastern region, where it is often seen basking on floating logs. Lays 7–13 soft-shelled eggs in spring.

YELLOW-BELLIED TERRAPIN *Pelusios castanoides* 18–23cm

A terrapin of the eastern coastal areas, with an elongate, smooth dark brown shell and *small plastral hinge*. The plastron scutes are *yellow with faint dark markings on the front*. The dark head has *fine yellow spotting*. This terrapin shelters underground during droughts, and prefers shallow

water in lowland swamps. It feeds on small frogs and invertebrates caught among water weed. Females lay up to 25 eggs in early summer.

COMMON MARSH TERRAPIN *Pelomedusa subrufa* 15–20cm

This terrapin is the most widespread in the subcontinent, although absent from much of South Africa. The *hard shell is very flat* and has no *hinge on the plastron*. The neck is withdrawn sideways into the shell. There are *2 soft tentacles on the chin*. These

 terrapins inhabit pans, vleis and slow-moving rivers throughout southern Africa. When the pans dry, the terrapins leave the water and dig into moist soil beneath cover. They eat almost anything, including small birds coming to drink. It usually lays 10–20 soft-shelled eggs on a sandbank.

CAPE MARSH TERRAPIN *Pelomedusa galeata* 25–32cm

 This characteristic terrapin of South Africa is very similar to the Common Marsh Terrapin (above), but grows much larger and often has *2 small temporal scales* on each side of the head. In adults the *shell turns much darker, almost black*. These terrapins inhabit pans and pools in ephemeral rivers in South Africa, usually where crocodiles are absent. They can be found far from water at the start of the summer rains, looking for small pans to colonize. They eat a wide variety of small insects and frogs, and will also gulp floating dead insects from the water surface. Females come on land and lay up to 20 soft-shelled eggs in summer.

SOFT-SHELLED TERRAPINS Family Trionycidae

These are unusual terrapins with only 3 toes on each foot and a soft, leathery shell. A bony layer is still present beneath the skin. They are restricted mainly to Asia and North America, with only 5 species in Africa.

ZAMBEZI SOFT-SHELLED TERRAPIN
Cycloderma frenatum   35–50cm

A *large* species with a *very long neck* and *'snorkel-like' nose*. When withdrawn into the shell, the *hindlimbs are protected by flexible flaps*. This terrapin grows to 14kg, and uses its strong forelimbs to dig in soft mud for snails and mussels, which it crushes with its strong jaws. Lays clutches of 15–22 hard-shelled eggs in summer. This species is locally restricted to the Save River system of the Mozambique floodplain.

NILE SOFT-SHELLED TERRAPIN *Trionyx triunguis*   60–106cm

Olivier Pauwels

A *very large* species with a *very long neck* and *'snorkel-like'* nose. The withdrawn hindlimbs are *not covered by flexible flaps*. The shell is dark olive, usually with small white or yellow spots. This species grows to 60kg. As well as fish and aquatic invertebrates, it also eats palm nuts and fruit. Females lay up to 60 hard-shelled eggs in a sandbank in summer. Locally restricted to the mouth of the Kunene River in northern Namibia.

LAND TORTOISES Family Testudinidae

These are advanced chelonians that withdraw the head backwards into the shell. The hindfeet are elephant-like and they walk on the tips of the heavily armoured forefeet. All are terrestrial, laying hard-shelled eggs. Southern Africa has the richest diversity of tortoises in the world, with 14 species present.

GREATER PADLOPER *Homopus femoralis*

 10–14cm

A small tortoise but nonetheless still the *largest padloper*. The *shell is not hinged* and has a *small nuchal scale* and *paired gulars*, and *usually only 11 marginals*. The forelimbs have *only 4 toes* and a *buttock tubercle is present* on each thigh. The flattened shell is olive to rich red-brown, often with a wide black margin on each scute in juveniles. Males have longer tails but lack a concave belly. This species inhabits the highveld and rocky montane grassland, where it shelters in burrows or under large stone slabs. Lays 1–3 oval, hard-shelled eggs in summer.

PARROT-BEAKED TORTOISE *Homopus areolatus*

7–10cm

A smaller relative of the Greater Padloper (above) that has a similar shell and also only *4 toes on the forefeet*. However, the shell margins are usually *indented*, and the *dorsal scutes often have depressed centres*. Shell abnormalities are common. The *beak is strongly hooked* (hence

common name) and the nostrils open high on the snout. *Buttock tubercles are absent*. Breeding males have bright orange noses. Rarely seen, it remains within cover to avoid predation by crows, jackals and other predators. Lays 2 or 3 small eggs in a small hole dug in sandy soil. This species is restricted to the southern Cape.

KAROO/BOULENGER'S PADLOPER
Homopus boulengeri

10–14cm

Another small padloper, but with *5 toes on the forefeet*. The flattened shell has a *rounded bridge* and usually *12 marginals*. The *beak is only weakly hooked* and there are *no buttock tubercles*. The shell varies in colour from olive to rich red-brown. Males are smaller than females

and have a pronounced hollow belly. This tortoise is very secretive, and favours rocky ridges in the Karoo, where it shelters under large rock slabs. It is usually seen on cool summer days when thunderstorms approach. Lays a single, round, hard-shelled egg in a well-drained, sunny spot. May lay 2 or 3 eggs each year. **NT**

SPECKLED PADLOPER *Homopus signatus*

6–9cm

The world's smallest tortoise, with a flattened pale brown shell that is *heavily speckled* and has *serrated edges*. The shell in southern populations has smoother edges and a rich orange-red colour. There are *5 toes on the forefeet*, usually *12*

marginals, and *buttock tubercles are present*. Males are smaller than females and have a pronounced hollow belly. This tortoise can be found among the granite outcrops of Little Namaqualand, where it lives in small burrows excavated under a large rock slab, emerging in the early morning to feed on small succulent plants. Lays a single egg 2–4 times during summer. **V**

ANGULATE TORTOISE *Chersina angulata* 15–25cm

The only local tortoise that has an *undivided gular scute* beneath the throat. This is larger in males and is used in combat to overturn opponents. A *nuchal scute is present*, the *carapace has no hinge*, and there are *no buttock tubercles*. The shell is pale straw-yellow in colour with dark edges to the scutes.

The shells of old adults become smooth and dirty straw in colour. Some specimens, particularly from the Western Cape, have bright red bellies (the 'rooipens' form). Males are larger, and have a pronounced 'peanut'-shape and a hollow belly. This species is found throughout the Cape coastal regions, extending inland into succulent and broken karroid veld. The female lays a single, large egg at 4–6-week intervals during summer.

LEOPARD TORTOISE *Stigmochelys pardalis* 30–45cm

The largest tortoise in southern Africa, easily distinguished by the *lack of a nuchal scute* at the front of the shell. The *gulars are divided*, the *carapace has no hinge*,

and there are *2 or 3 buttock tubercles* on each side. Hatchlings are bright yellow, each scute with 1 or 2 black spots. Adults become darker and heavily blotched or streaked. Very old tortoises are almost uniformly dark grey. Males have longer tails and hollow bellies. This species is found throughout the region, but is absent from the grasslands of the highveld, succulent Karoo and Namib Desert. Lays up to 6 clutches of 6–15 eggs in summer.

GEOMETRIC TORTOISE *Psammobates geometricus* 8–12cm

A Critically Endangered tortoise, restricted to coastal renosterbosveld in the southwestern Cape. Only 2,000–3,000 specimens survive in a number of special reserves. It is the only tent tortoise found in fynbos habitat. The shell is *high and domed*, with only *slightly upturned rear margins*. The

marginal scutes along the bridge are higher than they are broad. There is a *small nuchal* and *single axillary*, but *no buttock tubercles*. The scutes of the shell usually have bright, radiating yellow and black rays. Females are larger and have smaller tails than males. Lays a small clutch of 2–4 eggs in spring, which hatch in late summer. **CE**

KALAHARI TENT TORTOISE *Psammobates oculiferus* 8–12cm

The low, domed shell, with *strongly serrated front and rear margins*, is characteristic. The *nuchal is broad* and *often divided*. Like in other tent tortoises, each shell scute has a radiating pattern of 6–10 dark

rays on a tan or pale brown background. *Buttock tubercles are present* and there is only a *single axillary scale*. Males have longer tails, more conical scutes on the back, and hollow bellies. The shell was often used by bushmen to make buchu pouches. This tortoise is found throughout the Kalahari region, where it feeds on small succulents and grasses. The female lays a small clutch of 1 or 2 eggs in summer.

TENT TORTOISE *Psammobates tentorius*   8–12cm

An attractive small tortoise that comes in a wide variety of shapes and colours. The shell usually has radiating black and yellow rays on each scute, although some specimens are uniformly brown. Each dorsal scute may be raised or flat, and the shell shape may be flattened or domed.

The *margins are not serrated*, and, unlike in the Geometric Tortoise (p.149), the *scutes along the bridge are broader rather than high*. This species occurs throughout the Karoo and southern Namibia, but is not easily found. Males are much smaller than females. Lays several 1–3-egg clutches in summer.

EASTERN HINGED TORTOISE *Kinixys zombensis*   17–20cm

Luke Verburgh

A medium-sized tortoise which, when adult, has a *characteristic hinge in the rear of the carapace*. This closes when it is disturbed to protect the hindfeet and tail. The carapace is *slightly domed* and the scutes have a radiating pattern of dark bands. *Adult males have a concave plastron.* This species is locally restricted to moist savanna and thicket of the eastern coastal plain, from Zululand north to East and West Africa. It emerges in the early morning and evening to feed on fruits and soft plants. It also eats snails and millipedes. Lays 2–7, exceptionally up to 10, eggs in summer.

NATAL HINGED TORTOISE *Kinixys natalensis* 8–14cm

A small species in which the *hinge is poorly developed* and *restricted to the marginals*. The *supracaudal is frequently divided*, the *beak has 3 cusps*, and the *plastron is not concave in males*. *Scutes on the back and belly have broad concentric light and dark zones*, although these may fade in old specimens. It inhabits dry, rocky areas, and hibernates under rocks from May to September. The diet is similar to that of Eastern Hinged Tortoise (p.150). Lays small clutches of 1 or 2 eggs in summer, which take 5–6 months to hatch.

SPEKE'S HINGED TORTOISE *Kinixys spekii* 13–18cm

Another small species, with a *flattened shell* that allows it to seek refuge in rock cracks and hollow logs. The *beak has only 1 cusp*, the carapace *has a well-developed hinge*, and the *tail ends in a spine*. Breeding *males have a well-developed concave plastron*. These tortoises spend the dry season in woodland, moving to more open savanna to feed on small annuals after the summer rains. They also readily eat fungi and snails, and especially millipedes. Lays a small clutch of 2–4 eggs in summer.

SEA TURTLES Superfamily Chelonioidea

Sea turtles have front feet that are modified into flippers, and they are unable to withdraw the head or feet into the shell. They are found throughout tropical seas, but return to sandy beaches to lay their soft-shelled eggs. Five species are found in the region's coastal waters, with 2 nesting on protected beaches in northern Zululand.

GREEN TURTLE *Chelonia mydas* 98–120cm

A non-breeding visitor to the eastern and western coasts, where it enters shallow estuaries to feed on sea grasses and jellyfish. The hard shell is *smooth*, with *non-overlapping scutes*. There are *12 marginals on each side*, which are smooth in adults. The front flippers have a *single claw*. Females are usually darker in colour than males. They are slow-growing, taking 10–15 years to mature. These turtles are threatened by pollution and by slaughter for their meat and eggs. The nearest nesting beaches are on the Tanzanian coast. **NT**

HAWKSBILL TURTLE *Eretomochelys imbricata* 60–90cm

A non-breeding visitor to the east coast. The hard shell has *thick, overlapping scutes*. There are *12 marginals on each side*, the posterior markedly serrated. The front flippers have *2 claws*. This relatively small turtle feeds on corals and urchins that are prised from the bottom with the hooked beak. Many millions have been killed for their shells, which are used as the famous 'tortoiseshell' in fashion. The nearest breeding grounds are in northeastern Madagascar and Mauritius. **NT**

LOGGERHEAD TURTLE *Caretta caretta*   70–100cm

Johan Marais

A frequent visitor to the east coast that breeds on the protected beaches of northern Zululand. It is a large turtle, with a *big head* and an elongate shell that tapers at the rear. The shell scutes are *smooth* (*keeled* in hatchlings), *non-overlapping*, and each limb has *2 claws*. Both adults and young are brown. The strong jaws are used to crush crabs, molluscs and sea urchins, which form the main diet. This turtle hunts around reefs and rocky estuaries. Females come ashore on dark nights and lay up to 500 eggs in clutches of about 100 at 15-day intervals. About 400–500 females nest in Zululand each year. **V**

LEATHERBACK TURTLE *Dermochelys coriacea*   130–170cm

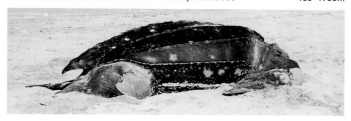

Found around the coast, and breeding on the northern Zululand beaches. It is the largest sea turtle, easily recognized by the *pliable, rubbery shell*, which has *12 prominent ridges*. The young are blue-grey and have *long flippers*. This turtle is a specialist feeder on jellyfish, voyaging the ocean currents in search of its prey. It may dive to depths of over 300m, spending up to 37 minutes underwater. Females come ashore at high tide on moonless nights between November and January. They dig a shallow pit and lay clutches of 100–120 eggs, up to 9 times in a season. Development is rapid; juveniles hatch after 70 days and head out to sea. Many get washed south in the Agulhas Current and strand on the Cape beaches. **E**

FURTHER READING

Alexander, G. and Marais, J. 2007. *A Guide to the Reptiles of Southern Africa*. Struik Nature, Cape Town.

Branch, Bill, 1998. *Field Guide to the Snakes and other Reptiles of Southern Africa*. rev. ed. Struik Publishers, Cape Town.

Branch, Bill, 2008. *Tortoises, Terrapins and Turtles of Africa*. Struik Nature, Cape Town.

Marais, J. 2004. *A Complete Guide to the Snakes of Southern Africa*. Struik Nature, Cape Town.

GLOSSARY OF TERMS

Apical pit   A sensory pit, paired or single, at the tip of the body scale of a snake.

Arboreal   Living in or among trees.

Bridge   The side of a chelonian shell where the carapace joins the plastron.

Carapace   The upper surface of a chelonian shell.

Caudal   Pertaining to the tail.

Chelonian   A shield reptile (tortoises, terrapins and turtles).

Clutch   All the eggs laid by a female at one time.

Cryptic   Hidden or camouflaged.

Dorsal   Pertaining to the upper surface of the body.

Dorsolateral   Pertaining to the upper surface of the body bordering the backbone.

Ectotherm   An animal, including all reptiles, that obtains its body heat externally, usually from basking in the sun.

Femoral   Pertaining to the upper part (thigh) of the hindlimb.

Granular   (of scales) Small, usually non-overlapping scales.

Hinge   A flexible joint in the shell of some chelonians.

Keel   A prominent ridge, occurring on the back of some chelonians, and on the scales of some lizards and snakes.

Plastron   The lower surface of a chelonian shell.

Scansor   Specialized scales found on the toe-tips of many geckos. They are covered in thousands of minute hairs that catch in cracks and allow the gecko to climb vertical surfaces.

Scute   An enlarged horny plate on a chelonian shell.

Squamate   A scaled reptile, including snakes, lizards and amphisbaenians.

Temporal   Pertaining to the side of the head behind the eye.

Tubercle   An enlarged scale on the body of a lizard.

Ventral   Pertaining to the lower surface of the body.

Vestigial   Being smaller and of a simpler structure (a remnant) than in an ancestor.

Head scales of a typical snake

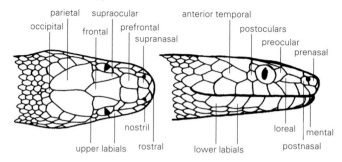

parietal
occipital
supraocular
frontal
prefrontal
supranasal
anterior temporal
postoculars
preocular
prenasal
nostril
upper labials
rostral
lower labials
loreal
mental
postnasal

Colour patterns of a lizard

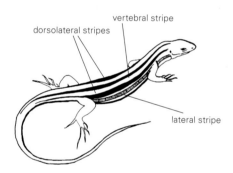

vertebral stripe
dorsolateral stripes
lateral stripe

Tortoise shields

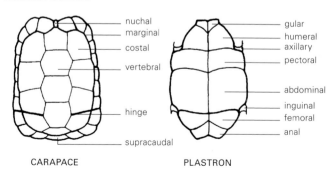

nuchal
marginal
costal
vertebral
hinge
supracaudal
gular
humeral
axillary
pectoral
abdominal
inguinal
femoral
anal

CARAPACE

PLASTRON

INDEX TO COMMON NAMES

SNAKES

CHELONIANS

INDEX TO SCIENTIFIC NAMES

SNAKES

CHELONIANS